Railroad Stations,
Depots & Roundhouses

Railroad Stations,
Depots & Roundhouses

Michael Golay

BARNES
&NOBLE
BOOKS
NEW YORK

This edition published by Barnes and Noble, Inc., by arrangement with Saraband Inc.

2000 Barnes & Noble Books

Design copyright © 2000 Ziga Design

Photography copyrights: Please see page 144 for photo credits and copyrights

Library of Congress Cataloging in Publication Data available

ISBN: 0-7607-2027-4

Printed in China

10 9 8 7 6 5 4 3 2 1

Page 1: *Winged Mercury presides over the entrance to New York City's newly restored Grand Central Terminal.*

Page 2: *Arches flank the broad curved entryway leading to Daniel Burnham's Pennsylvania Station in Pittsburgh, opened in 1903. A multistory railroad office building rises behind the archways.*

Right: *Architect Frank Furness designed the 1891 addition and ornate interior spaces of Broad Street Station in Philadelphia. Nearly 600 trains a day once called at Broad Street; the last pulled out on April 26, 1952.*

Contents

Introduction: The Railroad Age

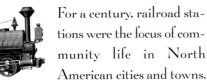

For a century, railroad stations were the focus of community life in North American cities and towns. Railroads accelerated the process of settlement, urbanization and industrialization of the nineteenth-century United States and Canada. They brought in crowds and goods, strangers and new things; they linked large places to small; they knocked down barriers of isolation; they helped create a national consciousness and a national economy. In Ralph Waldo Emerson's phrase, railroads were like a "magician's rod" in their power to "evoke the sleeping energies of land and water."

Tens of thousands of passenger depots were built in the United States between 1830 and 1955. Most early stations were flimsy things, built of wood and thus susceptible to a stray spark from a coughing locomotive; a new depot in East Boston burned to the ground the day it opened in 1845. With the railroads' economic decline, stations in many places crumbled into dust through disuse and neglect. Hard times threatened even the grandest of terminals. Majestic Pennsylvania Station in New York City, opened in 1910 with an interior modeled on the Roman Baths of Caracalla, fell to the wrecker's ball in the 1960s. Many others survived only by conversion to other uses. In 1999 a museum called Science City opened in Kansas City's now-quiet Union Station, the second-largest depot in America.

The first few miles of the Baltimore & Ohio Railroad, which would become America's first trunk line, opened in May 1830, using horses for motive power. In August of that year, Peter Cooper's *Tom Thumb* steam engine pulled a train of cars along the B&O route west from Baltimore, reaching an astonishing speed of 18mph. More or less simultaneously, railroads with primitive locomotives and cars shaped like stagecoaches came into operation in New York, New Jersey and South Carolina. The Railroad Age had begun.

Opposite: *A sturdy brick passenger branch line station served the central New Jersey town of Pemberton. Quiet today, the depot was once a nerve center of Pemberton, its main link to the outside world.*

Below: *Philadelphia-born architect Frank Furness modified his city's Green Street Station in his famous Eclectic Gothic style for the Philadelphia and Reading Railroad (c. 1885).*

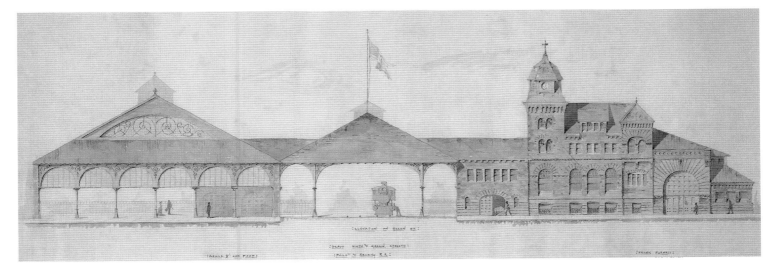

The first halts, or depots, in the United States and Canada were indistinguishable from other commercial buildings. Trains ran down the center of a town's main street and stopped for passengers at principal intersections, or in front of a hotel or a stagecoach office. Houses, shops, markets and hotels were adapted for railroad purposes. From 1835 to 1850, the B&O used a converted three-story brick house, once a tailor's quarters, for its Washington, D.C., station.

As a functional building, the railroad station had no precedent, so it had to be invented. A distinct "railroad style" soon evolved. Initial tastes in America ran to familiar forms that aimed to "comfort and reassure those concerned about the newness of it all," as historians Jeffrey Richards and John MacKenzie noted in *The Railroad Station: A Social History* (1986). As the century wore on, architects and railroad company engineers worked from European models—

Italianate, Gothic Revival, Romanesque, Renaissance, Eclectic—to develop hybrid styles wholly of the New World.

The following pages illustrate the major types of stations and the full range of building styles, from understated Greek Revival to florid Beaux-Arts. The first permanent urban stations went up in the 1830s. America's first purpose-built depot, the B&O's Mount Clare Station in Baltimore, showed its descent from a turnpike toll house. (The well-known brick polygonal structure that stands today replaced the original Mount Clare Station around 1851.) Tickets for the excursion to Relay, Maryland, could be purchased at Mount Clare, but the B&O provided no shed to house the train, nor a covered porch to shelter passengers. Small-town stations were simple cottagelike buildings with overhanging eaves. Country halts were more basic still, as Charles Dickens remarked

Below: *Builders ornamented this otherwise plain early station at Sudbury Junction, Ontario, with vertical and horizontal wooden sheathing. The city of Sudbury was the center of Canada's largest mining region.*

caustically in his travel narrative *American Notes* (1842): "The train calls at stations in the woods," he wrote, "where the wild impossibility of anybody having the smallest reason to get out is only to be equalled by the desperate hopelessness of there being anybody to get in."

Temple styles were fashionable with the more ambitious railroad companies during the early years. For its new station at Lowell, Massachusetts, in 1835, the Boston & Lowell built a small temple with four columns under a pediment at each end and ten columns along the sides. In more modest places, such as Frederick, Maryland, the wooden "train barn" served the purpose well enough. The B&O station and train shed there formed one compact block; trains entered through a yawning barn-like doorway in the center of the building.

By 1840 more than 3,000 miles of track had been laid in the United States. The railroads were beginning to conquer time, distance, mountain and water barriers—even the weather. Boston had become America's first rail center, with six stations for six lines leading inland in every direction. The first Midwestern railroads

were in operation. Railroad buildings began to reflect the expanding importance of railroads in American life, though travelers from abroad still found most U.S. stations inadequate by European standards. In the United States and Canada, long distances and rough terrain meant that railroads expended resources first on equipment, track, bridges and viaducts rather than on impressive terminal facilities.

Architect Henry Austin's startling New Haven station, an Italianate building with a campanile and Moorish details, opened in 1849, the first important American station in the railroad style. It proved more imposing as a monument than efficient as a passenger depot. New Haven built a new one in 1874, though Austin's building survived as a market until July 4, 1896, when a fire consumed it.

During the 1850s, stations became standardized, with larger waiting rooms and improved amenities. In larger communities, two-sided stations, with separate platforms for arriving and departing trains, gradually superseded the type in which all traffic used a single platform alongside the building, and passengers were

Above: *The steam ferry terminal at Wilson Point, Norwalk, Connecticut, shown in this 1882 photo, connected the New England railroad network to the Long Island Railroad on the north shore of Long Island.*

Right: *A freight and baggage cart frames the nine-over-nine window sash of the little way station of Apohaqui, New Brunswick.*

Opposite above: *A statuary group surmounts the triumphal façade of Grand Central Terminal in New York City, a Beaux-Arts masterpiece of 1913. Monumental styles of the last great age of station-building reflected North American railroads' power, wealth and prestige.*

Opposite below: *The former Union Pacific depot of Caliente, Nevada, opened in 1923, is now a city hall. Conversion to new uses—museums, restaurants, shops, offices—has been the salvation of many small-town depots.*

obliged to cross multiple sets of track to reach their trains. The first "head" stations, with "stub-end" tracks perpendicular to the main structure, were built. This eventually would become the dominant form. In nearly all early stations, public spaces and offices were laid out parallel to the tracks. Most larger stations had a covered access to the trains.

More than 20,000 miles of track were laid in the United States between 1850 and 1860, bringing the aggregate network from the Atlantic to the Mississippi River to 30,626 miles. The telegraph, first tested in 1844 along the B&O right-of-way between Washington and Baltimore, now controlled the movements of trains. More powerful locomotives, more comfortable cars, and improved track and bridges permitted greater speeds and expanded service. People traveled farther, faster and more often than ever before. The rails had made a national commerce possible.

The Civil War of 1861–65 temporarily slowed railroad expansion, though groundbreaking for the first transcontinental line took place in December 1863. Railroads grew rapidly in the postwar years. They led the development of the West, calling cities and towns into being out of a vast empty landscape. New stations were built in hundreds of American and Canadian communities. Architect Henry Holly's "Design 34," published in his *Country Seats* of 1865, foreshadowed the late-nineteenth century synthesis of revivalist styles known as Eclecticism. He suggested an Italian villa with steeply pitched roofs and Victorian Gothic touches for country stations, for "they set a good architectural example and result in improving the taste of the community." Cornelius Vanderbilt's first monumental Grand Central Depot in New York City, modeled on the Palace of the Louvre, opened in 1871. It was the first important head station: a massive façade fronting a 600-foot-long, 200-foot-wide, iron and glass train shed covering multiple tracks and platforms—reportedly the largest interior space in America.

So the depot assumed its place as the central institution of cities and towns. The station agent rose to the dignity of an important personage. In small places, he handled all the jobs, from

selling tickets and operating the telegraph to splitting wood, pumping water and feeding the stove. However modest his duties, he had charge of the most important building in town, and often doubled as postmaster, express agent and real estate broker as well.

The first Pullman sleeping car rolled out of Chicago in 1859, bringing comfort and style to overnight travel. Within a decade or so, Westinghouse airbrakes and more efficient couplers and buffers made cars safer and smoothed out the ride. The railroads introduced standard time in 1883, dividing the United States into four zones. Along with the school bell and the factory whistle, depot clocks conditioned people in thousands of communities to "man's time." By the mid-'80s, long-distance trains were equipped with dining cars. U.S. lines to the Pacific were completed in 1869, 1881 and 1883. The first Canadian Pacific Railway train reached Vancouver, British Columbia, in 1886.

Station-building continued apace. A depot's size and design usually reflected the importance,

or anyway the pretensions, of the place it served. In the West, the Union Pacific built stations of a standard pattern to replace the shacks, log huts and refitted box cars of pioneering days. In the settled East, the architect Henry Hobson Richardson's Romanesque buildings, with their heavy masses of stone, arches and towers, set the fashion for a time; good examples survive in New London, Connecticut, and North Easton, Massachusetts. Grander stations went up in larger places. Stylish Park Square Station in Boston, all tall towers and gables, won acclaim as a masterpiece of the 1870s. Inside were a large waiting room with rose windows and clusters of gaslights, and such amenities as reading and billiard rooms. Imposing new stations were built in Worcester, Massachusetts; Indianapolis; Louisville, Kentucky; and Providence, Rhode Island. The Romanesque Union Station in St. Louis, opened in 1894, advertised itself as "the largest depot in the world." Such monuments stood out among America's claims to a new era of architectural distinction.

"Railway termini and hotels are to the nine-teenth century what monasteries and cathedrals were to the thirteenth century," the architectural journal *Building News* commented in 1875. "They are truly the only real representative buildings we possess. Our metropolitan termini have been leaders in the arts and spirit of our time."

The last great phase of American station-building began in the 1890s. Carroll Meeks, in *The Railroad Station: An Architectural History*, called the new style "megalomania," a grandiose expression of America's new standing as a world political and economic leader. A politer term is Beaux-Arts, a blend of classical and Renaissance features expressed triumphally. Railroads reached the apex of their wealth and power around the turn of the twentieth century, and monumental new urban stations reflected their unchallenged status. The number of railroad companies peaked at 1,504 in 1907; railroad employment reached a new height of 1.7 million workers in 1910.

Developers of Washington, D.C.'s, Union Station, opened in 1907, overbuilt deliberately

Below: *A welcome arch leads to the 1915 Beaux-Arts façade of Denver's Union Station, built in 1881. The city demolished the arch, a landmark for three generations of travelers, in 1931.*

in anticipation of crowds for quadrennial presidential inaugurations. Pennsylvania Station, opened in 1910, covered 28 acres in the heart of midtown Manhattan. The second Grand Central Station, opened in 1913, had a concourse 125 feet wide, 375 feet long and 120 feet high, with a dazzling blue-and-gold zodiac mural on the curved ceiling. Some sixty-seven tracks accommodating 600 trains and 110,000 passengers a day led into Grand Central. The main façade of Toronto's Union Station, opened in 1927, extended more than 700 feet, with twenty-two unfluted Doric columns in Indiana limestone along part of its frontage.

By the time the Prince of Wales dedicated Toronto's new station, the railroads' long slide had begun. Rural lines and country and small-town stations felt the effects first. A few large stations were built as railroad passenger service entered its twilight—Omaha in 1930, Cincinnati in 1933, Montreal in 1943. Most designs were geometrical and severely func-

tional, although Spanish Baroque and Mission styles enjoyed a late vogue in the South and West. The last large station in the United States to be completed before World War II opened in Los Angeles in 1939.

By the 1950s, such new depots as appeared were apt to be workaday complexes like the romantically named Route 128 Station near Boston, hardly more inspiring than a bus stop. Though many stations were refurbished for new uses in the 1970s and '80s, the prospect of demolition always loomed. Taking up large tracts of valuable city land, and too costly for financially strapped railroads to maintain, great cavernous stations became an endangered species. Wrecking crews struck down the magnificent Pennsylvania Station to make way for a sports arena and an office tower.

We will "be judged not by the monuments we built," *The New York Times* observed mournfully after Penn Station's fate had been decided, "but by those we have destroyed."

Above: *The Oregon Express prepares to charge out of the Central Pacific depot at Sacramento, California, in this 1882 photo. The Central Pacific met the Union Pacific at Promontory, Utah, in May 1869 to complete the first transcontinental railroad line.*

The Advent
of Steam

Baltimore merchants were losing their trade with the interior. Two leading businessmen, Philip E. Thomas and George Brown, just returned from England, called a meeting for February 12, 1827, to discuss means of recapturing the business of the interior from steamboats and canals. Thomas and Brown had investigated the English railways on the trip. By month's end, they and their partners had obtained a charter to build and operate a railroad that would run from Baltimore to the Ohio River.

The venerable Marylander Charles Carroll of Carrolton, the last surviving signer of the Declaration of Independence, laid the cornerstone of the Baltimore & Ohio, and by May 1830 the first 13 miles of track were open to Ellicott's Mills. The cars on what would become America's first common-carrier railroad were horse-drawn at first. Then the B&O experimented with a sail-powered car. When the winds proved fickle, the railroad turned to steam.

"I believe I could knock together a locomotive," the New York merchant/inventor Peter Cooper told the B&O directors.

On its first run, on August 28, 1830, Cooper's 1½-horsepower *Tom Thumb* engine pulled a car full of B&O investors west toward Ellicott's Mills, demonstrating that steam could power a railroad. The B&O introduced regular passenger service, using a more powerful locomotive, the *York*, which could reach speeds of 30mph on level track, in the summer of 1831. By then, railroads were in operation, under construction, or

in the planning phase in New Jersey, New York and South Carolina, and steam had won out decisively over horse and sail.

"There is no reason to expect any material improvement in the breed of horses in the future," observed railroad engineer Horatio Allen, arguing for the new technology in 1830, "while, in my judgment, the man is not living who knows what the breed of locomotives has placed at his command."

So the prophets and visionaries saw their dreams take form. "I do verily believe that carriages propelled by steam will come into general use and travel at the rate of 300 miles a day," Philadelphia inventor Oliver Evans asserted as early as 1813. Evans went on to propose a steam railroad to carry passengers and freight between New York and Philadelphia. As late as 1830, that 90-mile trip via ferry and stagecoach consumed an entire exhausting day. The Camden & Amboy Railroad, which introduced service between Raritan Bay and the Delaware River in 1832, reduced the time of the journey to seven hours. Charging a three-dollar fare, the Camden & Amboy carried 110,000 passengers during its first year.

In New York State, the 17-mile Mohawk & Hudson Rail Road opened between Albany and Schenectady in 1831. Railroads leading from Boston to Lowell and Worcester began operations in the early 1830s. Work on the Chesterfield Railroad of Virginia commenced around the same time. The Chesterfield's 13 miles of track ran from the coalfields at Falling Creek to the head of tidewater on the James River at Richmond. In

Opposite: *A station freight agent awaits the arrival of a Baltimore & Ohio passenger train at Ellicott City, Maryland, in this photo of about 1900.*

1833 the South Carolina Railroad stretched 136 miles from Charleston to Hamburg, making it the longest line in the world. Over a six-month period in 1836, the Charleston-Hamburg road carried 16,000 passengers.

Canada's first railroads, horse-drawn coal-haulers, opened in Nova Scotia in 1827 and 1828. The first steam road, the Champlain & St. Lawrence, began operations along 15 miles of track from Laprairie on the St. Lawrence River to St.-Jean on the Richelieu in 1836. Three years later, the Erie & Ontario connected Chippawa and Queenstown near Niagara Falls. But Canadian railroads developed slowly, with only 22 miles of track laid by 1848.

In the United States, railroads expanded despite formidable opposition, often from competing canal, turnpike and stagecoach interests, and sometimes from traditionalists who objected on general principles. A Boston journalist judged the projected line to Albany "as useless as a railroad to the moon." In Ohio, a school board resolved that railroads were "a device of Satan to lead immortal souls to hell." Teamsters stigmatized Massachusetts legislators as "cruel turnpike killers and despisers of horseflesh" for granting the state's first railroad charter.

The earliest railroad stations in North America were frame shacks or converted buildings. Rural stops were sometimes no more than a path leading to the tracks and a signpost. The Camden & Amboy line adapted an inn at Bordentown, New Jersey, for its Delaware River Terminal. The Delaware & Hudson Railroad took over a house for its first depot in Schenectady. For its first station in the Kentucky bluegrass country, the Lexington & Ohio leased space in the Lexington market house. Travelers learned to check billposters, hotel notice boards and newspaper advertisements for train-departure *places*. "A through train for the accommodation of Western Passengers will leave the vicinity of Broad and Callowhill St. [per] A. McHaffey Supt. Columbia & Philadelphia Rail Road," ran an 1837 ad in a Philadelphia paper. Schedules remained approximate, however, despite the confident tone of such notices as Canada's first rail timetable, published in the *Montreal Gazette* on July 23, 1833. The Champlain & St. Lawrence Railroad promised passengers that a combined steamer-locomotive service would leave Montreal for St. John's promptly at 8 o'clock a.m. Scheduled or otherwise, trains of the 1830s were so reliably late that the expression "to lie like a timetable" soon found its way into everyday speech.

The pioneering Baltimore & Ohio led the way in station-building, too. The B&O put up two of the earliest purpose-built stations in the United States: Mount Clare in Baltimore and the depot at Frederick, Maryland. The first Mount Clare, built in 1830, had no amenities for passengers other than a ticket window. The depot at Frederick took the form of a train barn, with a shelter for the engine and cars, but no services for passengers. It bore a strong resemblance to its agricultural model. "Except for the presence of trains instead of hay wagons," wrote the architectural historian Carroll Meeks, "a train barn was indistinguishable from a substantial farm barn."

The first passenger conveyances were patterned on stagecoaches. Longer enclosed coaches seating forty to sixty passengers evolved over time. They had central aisles, windows, an iron stove for heat and candles for light, but few other comforts. "The cars are like shabby omnibuses," Charles Dickens wrote disapprovingly, "only larger." Philadelphia merchant Samuel Breck evidently regarded a rail journey as a form of torture. "If one could stop when one wanted,"

Below: *In 1830, inventor Peter Cooper's* Tom Thumb *locomotive supplied conclusive evidence that steam could pull a train of cars.*

he wrote, "and if one were not locked up in a box with 50 or 60 tobacco-chewers; and the engine and fire did not burn holes in one's clothes...and the smell of the smoke, of the oil and of the chimney did not poison one...and one were not in danger of being blown sky high or knocked off the rails—it would be the perfection of traveling." Such improvements as swivels attaching four-wheeled trucks to the cars made for a smoother ride through curves. Link and pin couplings replaced the three-foot strands of chain that joined the earliest cars, eliminating the sharp jerk as the train started and the jarring thump as it shuddered to a stop.

The first railroads ordinarily offered two classes of service. The first-class fare from Boston to Albany on the Western Railroad in 1842 ran to $5.50; second-class passengers paid $3.66. North and South, the cars were commonly segregated by race. "A black man never travels with a white one," Dickens observed, "there is also a negro car; which is a great, blundering, clumsy chest, such as Gulliver put to sea in from the kingdom of Brobdingnag." Some Southern roads required African Americans to ride in baggage or freight cars. There were separate accommodations for women too, where smoking and chewing tobacco were prohibited and single men were barred from entry.

Technical innovations gradually made travel by train safer, faster and cheaper. Iron rails replaced wooden track with iron strips. Ballast under the track improved drainage and stability. Camden & Amboy engineers introduced a cowcatcher on their locomotive in 1831, reducing one major hazard of train travel, livestock straying onto the track. "That rig ought to impale any animal that may be struck and prevent it from falling under its wheels," remarked its inventor, C&A mechanic Isaac Dripps. A spark arrester atop the smokestack lessened another hazard— the risk of fire to woods, fields and wooden buildings along the route. The locomotive whistle made its appearance in 1837. By about 1840, kerosene-burning headlamps made night travel possible. Around that time, too, railroads began putting up warning signs at grade crossings:

"Look Out for the Engine while the Bell Rings," cautioned the Western Railroad in Massachusetts.

The early railroads poured capital into track, bridges, tunnels and equipment, leaving little left over for station buildings. The B&O opened a 37-mile branch line to Washington, D.C., in 1835, and the main line reached Harper's Ferry, now West Virginia, in 1839. The railroad built a famous S-shaped wooden bridge there. The approach to the Ohio ran through the mountains of West Virginia; B&O engineers rock-drilled eleven tunnels and erected 113 bridges along the route.

Engineer Charles Ellet, Jr. built cable suspension bridges over the Schuylkill River in Pennsylvania in 1842, the Niagara in upstate New York in 1847 and the Ohio at Wheeling, West Virginia, in 1849. James Kirkwood's Starucca Viaduct near Susquehanna, Pennsylvania, carried nearly a quarter-mile of track over seventeen bluestone arches 100 feet above the valley of Starucca Creek. Completed in 1848 at a cost of $320,000, it would win a place on the National Register of Historic Places in 1973 and remain in regular use into the 1990s.

Scattered building efforts were launched west of the Appalachians in the 1830s. Work on the first Ohio railroad, the Mad River & Lake Erie, began in 1835. The Galena & Chicago Union Railroad obtained a charter in 1836. As early as

Above: *This early steam engine saw service with the Natchez and Hamburg Railroad of Mississippi.*

Above: *Locomotives, like ships, were personalized with names. Here is the Baltimore & Ohio's* William Mason, *dating from the 1850s.*

1846, Asa Whitney of Michigan petitioned Congress for permission to build a railroad linking the Midwest to the Pacific.

As railroads expanded and their operations became more reliable, the need for depots, stations and terminals grew. Long, deep overhangs or eaves projecting over the platform to shelter passengers and freight from rain and snow began to appear at stations in all parts of the country. The Galena & Chicago built the first station in the boom city of Chicago. A long, low building with a cupola for train-spotting, it opened near Canal and Kinzie Streets in 1848. By then, depot-building was well advanced in the United States and Canada. The Lexington & Ohio built its first station at Lexington in 1835. A long, narrow two-story affair with a set of first-floor doors facing the tracks, the historic structure gave way to a parking lot in 1959.

The train shed, soon to be a characteristic feature of railroad architecture in larger places, first appeared in the United States at the depot in Lowell, Massachusetts, in 1835. Architect P. Anderson's drawings for the Lowell station and shed are the earliest surviving plans for such a structure. Within a decade or so, train sheds would evolve into separate buildings, massive vaulted structures with coverings for the cars and passengers. The first station at Syracuse, New York, with then-popular Greek Revival details, went up in 1838 over tracks that ran down the center of the city's main street. Utica, New York, built a station that was designed in the Greek temple style in the 1840s.

In Boston, America's first railroad capital, stations were substantially built of brick and stone even in the 1830s. Engineer/architect George Dexter's Haymarket Station, built in 1844–45, a large and imposing structure for its time, had a façade of ten Corinthian pilasters below a pediment, with a low wooden train shed spanning 78 feet. Designed with expansion in mind, the main building housed a carpet store on the upper floor. Kneeland Street Station of 1847, usually attributed to architect Gridley J.F. Bryant, "was the most completely equipped American station of the day," according to Carroll Meeks. The Old Colony Railroad's Boston terminus had a gaslit smoking room, barber shop, telegraph office, newsstand, lavatory, bootblack stand and baggage checkroom.

By the late 1840s, designs of later European origin were succeeding Greek and Roman temple styles. Rhode Island architect Thomas Tefft looked to Germany for the Romanesque design of his Providence Union Station of 1848. Tefft was only twenty-two years old when he built what is regarded as the first important American railroad station. In 1885, not long before Tefft's station burned to the ground, *American Architect* voted it one of the twenty best American buildings.

Henry Austin's fanciful New Haven station, an early example of what came to be called the "railroad style" in America, opened in 1849. Austin, a Connecticut native, served as a carpenter's apprentice as a youth and later worked in the office of architect Ithiel Town, where he picked up the basics of the profession. After he failed as a builder, Austin opened an architect's office in New Haven in 1837.

Austin adorned his depot with Moorish and Chinese details and a lofty campanile. A pagoda-style tower topped the long central block with its Italianate arcaded windows. Arresting as a monument, Austin's design turned out to be less than adequate for its purpose. He built the depot on two levels, with stairs leading from the waiting rooms down to narrow platforms in the cut. The oft-repeated story of the pious little boy traveling with his father illustrates the problem. The boy stepped out of the cars into a dark, gloomy, smoky cavern:

"Is this hell?" he asked his father.

"No, my son, New Haven."

The city was proud of its new station, though. *Benham's City Directory and Annual Advertiser* for 1849–50 provided this description:

"The beautiful edifice...is situated on Union Street and occupies the entire square from Chapel to Cherry Street being 300 feet in length. The style of architecture is Italian with a tower at each end...that to the north rises to an altitude of 140 feet above the pavement."

The *Directory* went on to describe the gentlemen's and ladies' parlors, "with a profusion of rich and costly sofas, divans, chairs, ottomans, mirrors, etc.," a clock with four glazed and gaslit faces, and, above the clock, a bell that rang to announce the arrival and departure of the trains and doubled as a fire alarm.

"Long may it stand," the *Directory* wound up, "as an enduring monument to the taste, the liberality, and the enterprise of its projectors."

The Baltimore & Susquehanna Railroad's Calvert Station in Baltimore, completed in 1848, was an Italianate design with similarities to Tefft's building in Providence. An early head-type station, in which the tracks came in at right angles to the main building, Calvert had a shed that extended the full width of the main block, sheltering five lines and three platforms.

By 1850 railroads were on the rise to a dominant place in North American life. As transportation, they had supplanted roads and canals. As social centers, railroad stations had become the hub of community life in hundreds of cities and towns. Track mileage in the United States more than doubled between 1840 and 1850, and would more than triple in the coming decade.

"I hear the whistle of the locomotive in the woods," Ralph Waldo Emerson wrote from Concord, Massachusetts, on the Fitchburg Railroad. "Wherever that music comes it has its sequel. It is the voice of the civility of the Nineteenth Century saying 'Here I am.'"

Left: *Architect Henry Austin borrowed liberally from Moorish and Chinese styles for the passenger station in New Haven, Connecticut, an early example of the "railroad style." The depot, which served the New York & New Haven Railroad, opened in 1849.*

An Early B&O Landmark

The venerable Baltimore & Ohio depot at Ellicott City, Maryland, opened about 1831 as a freight and engine house. It began handling passengers in 1856. Ellicott City, then known as Ellicott Mills, was the end of the line for America's first regularly scheduled passenger service, inaugurated in the 1830s from Baltimore 13 miles to the east. The photograph below dates from the 1950s; exterior details of the station building had hardly changed in half a century.

Baltimore's Railroad Heritage *Left and Below*
Mount Clare Station (left), originally polygonal in form,
opened about 1851 and was subsequently added to. The
Baltimore & Ohio established a railroad museum there in
1953. The Baltimore & Ohio Railroad's Camden Station
(below) dates from 1856, with the wings added in 1865.
The 185-foot-tall central tower shown here was once
Baltimore's tallest structure. It was cut down and replaced
with a cupola in the 1870s.

Historic Harpers Ferry *Above*

The depot at Harpers Ferry, West Virginia, at the confluence
of the Shenandoah and Potomac Rivers, served Baltimore
& Ohio mainline trains on east-west routes originating
in Baltimore. The small town (then located in Virginia)
became famous as the scene of John Brown's Raid on the
Federal arsenal here — a proximate cause of the Civil War.

Adaptive Reuse *Below*

This early Baltimore & Ohio station on East Martin Street in Martinsburg, West Virginia, opened in 1849 as the Berkeley Hotel. The B&O took over the building after Confederate troops burned the original station building during the Civil War. A roundhouse was added in 1866, and other buildings were subsequently erected at Martinsburg's station complex, as shown on pages 42–43.

An Early Freight Depot *Above*
The Housatonic Railroad's imposing barrel-vaulted freight station at Bridgeport, Connecticut, opened about 1850. The Housatonic was a division of the powerful New Haven & Hartford Railroad.

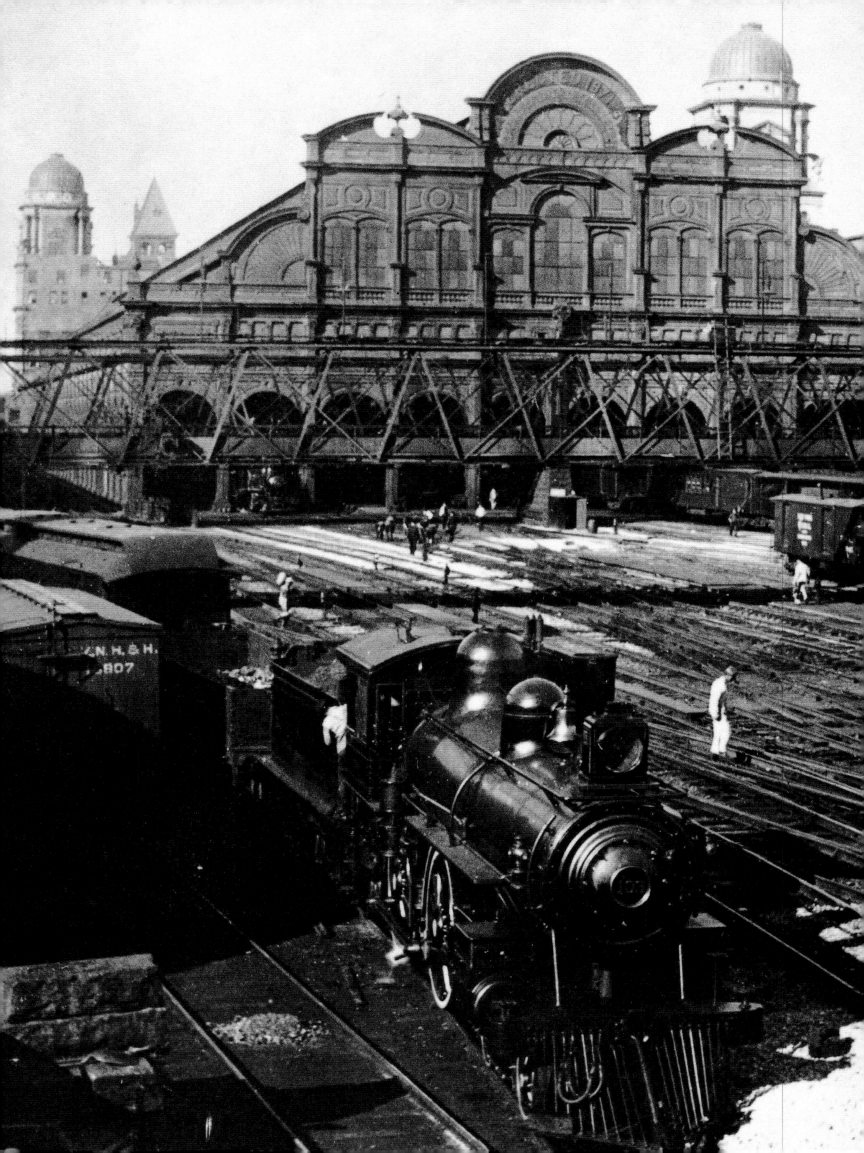

The Triumph of the Rails

The first copy of *American Railway Guide* appeared in 1850, listing a bewildering array of companies, routes and schedules along the nation's 8,879 miles of track. A journey of any distance required meticulous planning and not a little luck. How many changes? Where to break the trip for meals, or for a night's sleep? Above all, when to turn up at the depot, for the *Guide* gave train arrivals and departures in local times, variable, unsynchronized, keyed to a station agent's "turnip" (pocket watch), or an eccentric courthouse clock.

The railroads expanded and consolidated in spite of such obstacles. Axemen felled great swathes of forest to drive North America's wood-burning locomotives—U.S. railroads used an estimated 4–5 million cords a year during the 1850s. One could even travel for pleasure. Three-day train/steamboat excursions to the beauty spot of Niagara Falls were available for as little as $16.50 round trip. From June 1–4, 1857, politicians and railroad notables journeyed from Baltimore to St. Louis in a special train, with only a short break on an Ohio River steamboat, to mark the introduction of through service from the Atlantic to the Mississippi.

Equipment, bridges, roadbeds and signals lagged behind the pace of expansion, though, and the accident rate soared as a result. There were 138 train wrecks in 1853 alone. Illinois Central and Michigan Southern trains met in a thunderous collision at Grand Crossing near Chicago that year, killing eighteen passengers and crew and injuring forty. In 1856 a train packed with Sunday-school excursionists struck a freight train outside Philadelphia, touching off an explosion of the passenger locomotive's boiler. Fire spread to the highly combustible coaches, killing 62 travelers and injuring 100 in America's worst train disaster to that date.

All the same, the rails had become the dominant form of transportation in North America by 1860, when the U.S. network totaled 30,626 miles. The great railroad systems were forming. The Pennsylvania Railroad opened the first through line to Pittsburgh in July 1858 and continued its push westward into the 1860s, eventually reaching Chicago and St. Louis. The railroad also expanded 90 miles north and east from Philadelphia to the west bank of the Hudson opposite New York City. An innovative road, the Pennsylvania experimented with coal as locomotive fuel as early as 1853. It became the first U.S. line to lay steel rails, and most likely the first to use airbrakes on its trains.

A second great system of the northeastern United States, the New York Central, grew out of the consolidation in 1853 of ten short railroads in the Mohawk Valley/Erie Canal region of upstate New York. The merger, the work of a group of speculators led by the powerful iron manufacturer Erastus Corning, created a through line from Albany on the Hudson to Buffalo on Lake Erie—a total of 524 miles of track (including branch and spur lines) with a rolling stock consisting of 187 first-class passenger coaches and 1,702 freight cars.

The development of passenger stations and other railroad buildings during the 1850s reflected

Opposite: *The New York, New Haven & Hartford Railroad used the Park Avenue yards at the first Grand Central Terminal in New York beginning in 1872. This photo, looking from 46th Street, dates from 1889.*

◆ 27

the pre-eminence of the iron horse. Stations took on their familiar form in the years just before the Civil War. Great or small, most were the work of railroad-company engineers, and so were built to a practical pattern. In bigger, more prosperous places, architects designed the passenger areas, while engineers were responsible for the ever larger and more complex sheds covering both trains and platforms.

Specialized structures—roundhouses, machine shops, turntables, water tanks, crossing-guard shanties and signal towers—were grouped around or near major depots. Roundhouses were practical unadorned buildings for locomotive storage and repair. The restored roundhouse at the Steamtown National Historic Site in Scranton, Pennsylvania, is a typical example. They weren't invariably round, though: A three-quarter roundhouse survived in railroad use at Anaconda, Montana, into the 1990s.

Yardmen shifted engines weighing many tons on hand-powered turntables, wooden-truss affairs in the early days, later, of cast iron or steel. Engineer Gridley Bryant designed the first U.S. turntable for the horse-drawn Granite Railroad of Quincy, Massachusetts. Most early locomotive turntables were of the "armstrong" type that required human motive power. As larger locomotives entered into service, turntable design improved. The Philadelphia & Columbia Railroad replaced an inadequate wooden table with a 50-foot iron model in 1855. A P&C enginehouse offi-

cial declared himself well pleased with the new device: "The table is made of cast-iron...with Parry's anti-friction box, or pivot, of which I cannot speak too highly," he wrote. "No gearing is required, and two men can turn the heaviest locomotive in one-third the time that half a dozen men could with the old arrangement."

Italianate forms remained fashionable among station designers of the 1850s. The B&O's Italian Villa-style station in Washington opened in 1851. President-elect Abraham Lincoln stepped out of the train there for his first inaugural in 1861. Three slender towers rose above Baltimore's Camden Station of 1853 (shown in chapter 1), the central one surmounting a massive pediment. Inside were waiting rooms, a refreshment salon and railroad offices. Gothic Revival designs began to appear here and there. An early example, the depot at West Brookfield, Massachusetts, opened about 1847 as a scheduled eating stop on the Western Railroad. The wooden building with Gothic panels and tracery on the doors and windows survives today as a privately owned warehouse. Solomon Roberts, chief engineer of the Fort Wayne & Chicago Railroad, built a gabled stone station with a castellated tower in Alliance, Ohio, in 1853. The Philadelphia & Erie depot in Erie, Pennsylvania, dating from the early 1860s, had Gothic detailing about the windows and a stubby clock tower.

Smaller cities built "union" stations—those serving more than one railroad line. The first Union Station in Columbus, Ohio, opened in 1862. A wood-frame board-and-batten building with Gothic touches, it was a greatly expanded version of the train barn of early railroad days. Entire towns developed around railroad complexes in strategic locations. The Pennsylvania Railroad laid out Altoona, Pennsylvania, in 1849 as a switching point for locomotives preparing to climb into the Alleghenies. In 1854 the railroad opened the great "S" curve at Altoona, an engineering marvel that made the route through the mountains possible. The Logan House, billed as "one of the finest hotels in the U.S.," arose beside the flourishing Altoona station.

Below: *A few finishing touches remain before the Queen City station and hotel in Cumberland, Maryland, will be ready to receive travelers. This photo dates from 1872, just before the red brick Italianate depot/resort opened for business. The building lived for a century: wreckers knocked it down in 1972 to make way for a prefabricated Amtrak station.*

The Hudson River Railroad's terminal at Tenth Avenue and 30th Street in New York City opened in 1861 as one of the last of the one-sided big city stations. A *New York Tribune* reporter judged the new structure serviceable, if underwhelming. All the same, he supplied a detailed description of the station (which survived for only a decade):

"It is not a very imposing structure though well adapted for the purpose for which it was designed," *The Tribune* wrote. "It is of brick, is 200 feet long by 28 feet in width, with a roof projecting 15 feet over the platform in the rear. There are two entrances in front, one for ladies and one for gentlemen. At the east end is the ladies' sitting room and toilet occupying one-third of the building. West of the ticket office is the gentlemen's room, telegraph office and baggage room."

On balance, taking the good with the bad, American station design failed to impress architect Henry Holly. "In Britain, stations are beautiful and tasteful just as their trains are safe and luxurious," Holly wrote; he found American stations "uninviting or ridiculous, beggarly or pretentious." His all-purpose "Design 34" for railroad stations proposed an eclectic remedy blending Italian and Victorian Gothic elements. The unknown builder of the Old Colony Railroad station at Taunton, Massachusetts (1865), may have found inspiration in Holly's scheme. A stone building with a tower topped by a steep pyramid, Taunton's Gothic depot showed Holly's influence, if only indirectly.

Railroads and their buildings proved readily adaptable for military purposes, as the high strategists of nations soon discovered. Canadian legislation of 1851 mandated a wide 5-foot, 6-inch track gauge expressly aimed at blocking an American invasion via the rails. The law remained on the books until 1870. By then, Americans had fought the first railroad war. The Confederate army used Virginia rails to move troops to the battlefield as early as July 1861. Stations, other railroad buildings and even trains served as makeshift hospitals. Yankees and Rebels fought major battles for control of Manassas Depot in northern Virginia,

crossroads of the Manassas Gap and Orange & Alexandria Railroads.

Both sides targeted railroads for destruction. In its notorious campaigns in Georgia and the Carolinas in 1864–65, the Union army of General William T. Sherman demolished hundreds of miles of track. Sherman himself issued explicit orders about taking down depots and other railroad structures. "The railroad station as the heart of a modern artery of business was second only in importance to the buildings and institutions of the Confederate government itself, as a subject for elimination," he wrote later. The large terminal at Atlanta and a fine small depot at Millen, Georgia, were among the casualties of Sherman's March to the Sea.

While Union troops were industriously tearing up track and burning down stations in the South, railroad development proceeded in the North, though at a somewhat slower rate, given wartime demands on labor, materials and capital. Still, track, bridges, tunnels and stations continued to be built. Pittsburgh's Union Depot opened in 1865, the last year of the Civil War. The Atlantic & Great Western Railroad put up a fine Gothic Revival station at Meadville, Pennsylvania, in 1865. To a journalist from the New York *Herald*, the board-and-batten complex rivaled "in the style and beauty of its surroundings any of those you may notice in the best railroads of England; [with] charming cottages for the officers of the road, a park at the rear with winding walks, fir trees, rose and jessamine bushes." The Meadville depot also had a hundred-room hotel for its passengers, with "a dining room as long as a train."

The postwar years saw powerful Eastern financiers gain dominance over major railroad systems. As early as 1862, "Commodore" Cornelius Vanderbilt, the one-time ferryman who had become the richest man in America by 1850, acquired a controlling interest in the Harlem and the New York & Hudson Railroads, two small lines leading strategically from New York City toward Albany, the state capital. Vanderbilt then set about scheming to gain control of the New York Central. By the end of 1867, he had maneuvered himself into the presidency of the consolidated and temporarily renamed New York Central & Hudson. Over the next twenty years, he and his son William H. Vanderbilt would extend their railroad empire north into Canada and as far west as Chicago.

Construction of Vanderbilt's great New York City monument, the first Grand Central Depot at Fourth (now Park) Avenue and 42nd Street, commenced in 1869. His architect, John B. Snook, modeled the head house, built of iron, granite and brick, on the Parisian Palace of the Louvre. His engineers found inspiration for the cast-iron and glass train shed in London's St. Pancras Station (1863). The result: America's first palatial station, the equal of Europe's finest. The three tenant roads—the New York & Harlem, the New York Central and the New York & New Haven—had their own waiting rooms, ticket offices and baggage facilities. Twelve tracks ran into the high-vaulted, single-span shed, one of the largest in the world when it opened in December 1871. Grand Central soon became the second most-popular building attraction in the United States, after the U.S. Capitol in Washington, D.C.

In Chicago, America's rising second city, the Michigan & Southern and Rock Island depot (also known as LaSalle Street Station) had French Renaissance details as designed in 1870–71. It burned along with 17,000 other structures in the Great Chicago Fire of October 8–9, 1871. Completely rebuilt, the station reopened on October 25, 1872, with a series of band concerts in the train shed to celebrate the city's amazingly rapid reconstruction.

Railroads forced the pace of building and consolidation during the 1870s. Canada's railroad network grew from 2,065 miles in 1860 to nearly 12,000 miles in 1887. In the southern United States, railroad promoters rebuilt war-damaged lines and laid new ones. Northern financial houses assumed control of many Southern roads; even so, development lagged behind the North. The Louisville & Nashville took form as a major north-south artery, one of the few genuine through routes in the region. The grandly named "Great Southern Mail Route," for example, required many changes and stops and five full days to cover the distance between New York City and Mobile, Alabama. And the cost of train travel remained high throughout the states of the former Confederacy: about six cents per mile, double the rate in the North.

With the Pennsylvania and New York Central leading the way, Northern roads combined into large regional systems in the 1870s and '80s. The Boston & Maine, which would eventually operate 1,400 miles of track, grew out of the tiny Andover & Wilmington, chartered in 1833. The B&O extended its reach to Pittsburgh; Sandusky, Ohio; and Chicago. It adopted its famous emblem, the dome of the Capitol, in the 1880s. The Chicago & Northwestern succeeded a foreclosed road, the Columbus, Hocking Valley & Toledo, in 1889 and built up a network of 9,400 miles of track. In Canada, the Grand Trunk line operated nearly 2,600 miles of track in the late 1880s.

Consolidation encouraged standardization. Major railroads confronted the problem of time—in the 1870s, there were some eighty different zones in the United States, with countless local variations. Railroads operating in and out of Pittsburgh ran to six different times. Station clocks in Buffalo were set to three different times: that of the New York Central (New York City's), that of the Michigan Southern (Columbus, Ohio's), and local time. Philadelphia local time lagged five minutes behind New York City's. When noon struck in Chicago, it was already 12:09 PM in Louisville. There were at least thirty-eight local times in Wisconsin alone. Union Pacific trains operated on at least six different times as they steamed their way between Chicago and San Francisco.

The railroads' General Time Convention developed a standard system for the country in the early 1880s. At noon on Sunday, November 18, 1883, some 600 railroads simultaneously converted to standard time in four zones, Eastern, Central, Mountain and Pacific. At the West Side Union Depot in Chicago, which served four railroads, the stationmaster stopped the clock at 12:00 noon local time, then waited for a telegraphed report of high noon at the 90th meridian. That occurred at 12:09:32 by the agent's timepiece, at which time he restarted the station clock. From then on, the Western Union telegraph flashed out the correct time every Thursday at noon, when station clocks were duly recalibrated in depots from Maine to Texas and from New York to California.

"The sun is no longer boss of the job," the *Indianapolis Sentinel* observed. "People, 55,000,000 of them, must eat, sleep and work as well as travel by railroad time. It is a revolt, a rebellion. The sun will be requested to rise and set by railroad time. The planets must, in the future, make their circuits by such timetables as railroad magnates arrange."

In some locales, opposition to the arrangement provoked action as well as bitter words. The mayor of Bangor, Maine, vetoed an ordinance placing the city on standard time. "It is unconstitutional," the mayor declared, "being an attempt to change the immutable laws of God Almighty and hard on the workingman by changing day into night." Parsons denounced railroad time from their pulpits. A number of cities joined Bangor in resisting the change. Eventually, though, most of the country went along. A noteworthy exception: the United States government. Congress finally followed the railroads' lead in March 1918 with passage of the Standard Time Act.

No comparable public outcry accompanied the shift of most major railroads to standard track gauge. From the beginning, gauges had varied widely, from as narrow as two feet to as broad as six. Even connecting lines sometimes used different gauges. In mid-1886, major roads adopted the standard track gauge of 4 feet, 8½ inches between the rails. The Romans had used that gauge for chariot and cart rutways and, in the first century AD, for coal mines in Roman Britain. The British adopted the ancient standard for their mine railways and, eventually, for their steam railways too. In the United States, the conversion to standard gauge had the effect of drawing Southern railroads, many of which originally used a five-foot gauge, fully into the national system for the first time.

North and South, stations reflected railroad expansion. Big-city depots now offered a range of services, from meals and lodging to boot-blacking. The B&O and other major lines built hotels near or adjacent to major stations. A contemporary observer catalogued what the experienced traveler had learned to expect of the metropolitan terminal after several decades of steady development:

"The introduction at stations of placards announcing the arrival and departure of trains, the placing of clocks in conspicuous places, the employment of men to direct passengers, the establishment of bureaus of information, the institution of lunch counters and receptacles for packages, the placing of boxes into which complaints may be dropped, and many other conveniences were unknown in the early history of railroads, but are now regarded as essential, and have become, so to speak, public rights."

For large urban stations, architects borrowing freely from Gothic and Renaissance models created what amounted to an altogether new style that came to be called Picturesque Eclecticism. The High-Victorian head house of

Below: *Architect Gilbert Stanley Underwood designed the Art Deco-style Union Station at Omaha, Nebraska, which opened in 1931. The Union Pacific and six other railroads used the station in its prime; it closed in 1971.*

London's St. Pancras, with its turrets and tower and Gothic detailing about the windows and doors, influenced the design of Boston's Park Square Station, begun in 1872. Effective as a station, Park Square also would have made an excellent library, according to the *Library Journal* in 1879. All the same, Park Square fell to the wrecker's ball in 1899, six years after its services were shifted to the new South Station. An architectural commentator mourned the depot's passing, and provided a good description of the building at the same time: "It was long the show building of Back Bay. Its gentle English gothic exterior, its finely proportioned clock tower, and the atmosphere of elegant social intercourse which pervaded its waiting rooms, its exclusive barbershop and even its refined washrooms [were] wonderful."

The Baltimore & Potomac's Washington terminal opened in 1873, "an exceedingly handsome building," a contemporary thought, "and heated by steam throughout." An assassin shot and mortally wounded President James A. Garfield in the waiting room there on July 2, 1881. Union Station at Worcester, Massachusetts, built in 1875–77, served four rail lines—the Boston, Barre & Gardner, the Worcester & Nashua, the Providence & Worcester and the Boston & Albany. It was a handsome building too, with a graceful tower and slate-covered spire that rose to a height of 212 feet. The *Railroad Gazette* called the tower, head house and train shed together "the most picturesque structure of the kind which has yet been erected." The building reflected Worcester's pride, its sense of importance as a leading city of New England.

The architect Henry Hobson Richardson (1838–86), a Louisiana-born graduate of Harvard who later studied at the Ecole des Beaux-Arts in Paris, exerted an influence on American station design far out of proportion to the relatively modest number of small stations attributed to him. He refined Romanesque forms into a style that carried his name, Richardsonian, and in the process inspired a nationwide Romanesque revival that supplanted even Victorian Gothic in popularity. An

American Institute of Architects survey in 1885 chose five of Richardson's works for its list of the ten best American buildings. None of the selections was a railroad station; most of his designs were for small-town or suburban depots, with the exception of one of his last commissions—the brick Union Station in New London, Connecticut, completed in 1887. Even so, his work would influence a generation of railroad depot architects.

Richardson designed a series of stations in the Boston area, some of them in collaboration with the landscape architect Frederick Law Olmstead, the creator of Central Park in New York City. Richardson and Olmstead produced the Old Colony Railroad depot in North Easton, Massachusetts, a hip-roofed granite structure with brownstone trim and ornamental carved animals, including wolves, dragons and lions. All of his stations had key design features in common, as observed by the architectural historian William H. Pierson Jr.:

"[They] all had a low one-story block for a ticket office and waiting room, an open shed along the tracks, and a porte-cochère, with all the elements contained under a single hovering roof character," he wrote. "These charming little stations were all built of rock-faced masonry. Yet no two were alike." Richardson's followers spread his ideas across North America. His successors designed the Romanesque station at Springfield, Massachusetts (1889), in the master's manner. His influence on station design is also apparent in Indianapolis (1886–89), Louisville (1882–91), Hartford (1889) and St. Louis (1891–94). Canadian architects designed Richardsonian stations in Montreal (Windsor Station, 1888) and Toronto (1894).

Three major mid-Atlantic railroads, the Reading, the Pennsylvania and the B&O, commissioned the gifted Philadelphia architect Frank Furness (1839–1912) to design some 150 stations. Furness's distinctive Picturesque Eclectic style, with its blend of colors, textures and details from many periods, fell from favor during the twentieth century, and few of his railroad buildings still stand. His B&O station in Wilmington,

Delaware, with a multi-planed roof with projecting chimneys and dormers, survived in a dilapidated state into the late 1990s. Furness also designed the 1893 additions to the massive Broad Street Station in Philadelphia, opened in 1881. A grand staircase in solid marble led from the street level to the second floor, with its great open fireplace. The station restaurant, the Savarin, won a reputation as Philadelphia's finest. The train shed, 595 feet long and 300 feet wide, would turn out to be the largest ever built.

If railroads were a focus of community life in the closing decades of the nineteenth century, they were sometimes targets of resentment and even outrage, too, on account of their commanding place in the North American economy. "Charge all the traffic will bear" became the motto of many lines. The New York Central line's William H. Vanderbilt, the Commodore's son, really *did* say "The public be damned." Corruption and rate discrimination led to calls for state and, ultimately, federal regulation. Farmers, increasingly dependent on the rails to move their products, complained of extortionate freight charges and other sharp practices. America's nascent labor movement regarded the great railroad corporations as exploitative, sometimes blatantly so.

Many railroads cut wages and reduced spending for maintenance and equipment during the economic depression that followed the Panic of 1873, touching off strikes that led to rioting, property destruction and deaths in Baltimore, Pittsburgh and other railroad centers. The Pennsylvania Railroad led the way in June 1877, announcing a 10 percent pay cut even as it continued to pay generous dividends to stockholders. Other lines followed. Workers responded with protests here and there. One of the largest of the railroad craft unions, the Brotherhood of Locomotive Engineers, struck the Boston & Albany and the Philadelphia & Reading over wages. The P&R responded with an order to the line's engineers to quit the union or be fired.

Serious labor strife erupted with the B&O's notice on July 16, 1877, that it would slash pay by 10 percent. Firemen and brakemen in Baltimore petitioned management for a restoration, with no success. Some forty workers then walked off the job, tying up trains in Baltimore. Down the line at Martinsburg, West Virginia, striking workers prevented freight trains from clearing the yard. By July 18, 1,200 B&O freight cars were immobilized in Martinsburg.

The governor of West Virginia called out the militia. The citizen soldiers, sympathetic to the strikers, refused to break up the crowds. The strike spread to other B&O towns in West Virginia. More troops were called in, including U.S. regulars. Soldiers fired into a mob at Camden Junction, killing ten and wounding forty. The B&O refused strikers' offers to negotiate. With the aid of armed force, the railroad had broken the strike by August 1.

Meantime, Pennsylvania Railroad workers walked off the job in Pittsburgh. The company summoned troops, and twenty strikers and sympathizers were killed when soldiers fired into the crowd during a protest march down Liberty Street. A mob of 15,000, enraged, forced the troops to withdraw into the roundhouse at the

Below: *A rendering shows Broad Street Station in Philadelphia after architect Frank Furness's enlargement of 1891. The largest train shed ever built—300 feet wide and 595 feet long— stretched behind the station, which at its peak served 578 trains per day.*

Above: *Gravers Lane Station in Philadelphia was one of more than a hundred buildings architect Frank Furness designed for the Philadelphia & Reading Railroad in the 1880s, and is one of the few Furness structures still standing. The architect's Victorian idioms fell out of fashion in the early decades of the twentieth century.*

Pennsylvania's Pittsburgh yards. Rioters looted stores and set fires. One group lit off a coal-filled tender and rammed it through the brick wall of the roundhouse. The troops fought their way out of the burning building, firing indiscriminately as they went. Strikers set fire to a long line of rail cars outside the Union depot. The four-story station, an adjacent hotel and the Pennsylvania's office caught fire, and more than a hundred locomotives were damaged or destroyed. Damage to railroad and property in Pittsburgh exceeded $5 million.

Federal troops and the Coal & Iron Police finally quelled the mobs and restored order. With protection from some 10,000 soldiers, the Pennsylvania reported service restored all along the line by July 30. Strikes on the Erie, Lake Shore, New York Central and Michigan Central flared, then died out. Altogether, about 100 strikers and their allies were killed and 500 injured in the disturbances of 1877—one of the costliest explosions of labor violence in the history of the United States.

Unions probably emerged stronger from the strike, even though their immediate demands went unmet. Eugene V. Debs founded the American Railway Union in 1893 on a platform of higher wages and an eight-hour day. In 1894

the new union struck the powerful Great Northern Railroad. All 9,000 employees, including station agents, walked off the job. With operations at a standstill, the company capitulated after eighteen days. But when Debs's union struck the Pullman Company of Chicago later in the year, the railroads stood firm. With armed support from militia and federal troops, some twenty-four railroads operating in concert managed to keep the trains running, even those with Pullman cars. By August 2, the strike had been crushed. The Pullman shops reopened, and many striker activists were blacklisted from future railroad employment.

Railroads approached the apogée of their power, wealth and influence in the century's last decade. Rails reached into virtually every inhabited corner of America. Passenger travel neared its peak. Train travel had never been easier, safer, or more comfortable. The financiers launched another round of railroad consolidation in the 1890s, so that by 1906 seven groups would control roughly two-thirds of America's 225,000 miles of track. At the same time, the golden age of railroad expansion neared an end. Such new roads as were built were for commuters in the rapidly expanding suburbs, or for vacationers bound for lake, mountain and oceanfront resorts.

However, stations large and small continued to be built, and to define the places they served, presenting "at a glance something about [a community's] size, affluence, livelihood, and social range of the citizens," in the words of railroad historian Clay Lancaster.

Handsome new Union stations opened in Chicago in 1881 and in Baltimore in 1886. At Milwaukee's Gothic Union Station, finished in 1886, travelers approached the waiting room through a main entrance "formed of a triple arch supported by columns of polished granite...[with] swinging doors of polished oak a few feet inside the arch." Canada's Grand Trunk Railroad opened the French Renaissance Bonaventure Station in Montreal in 1887.

All the same, the railroad style in station-building was expending itself. Richardsonian influences were beginning to wane. Among the last of the great Romanesque designs were architect Theodore C. Link's vast Union Station in St. Louis and the Illinois Central depot in Chicago. Link's building claimed, for a time after it opened in 1894, to be "the largest depot in the world." A 230-foot-high clock tower rose from

a head house of brick clad with Indiana limestone. The cavelike interior, with a 606-foot-long Midway, induced feelings of awe, according to the architectural historian Carroll Meeks. The five-span train shed, 600 feet wide, covered some thirty lines leading into the station.

Architect Bradford Gilbert, the author of the *Sketch Portfolio of Railroad Stations*, privately published in 1881, designed the Illinois Central station. Work commenced on the complex's four components—train shed, tower, office building and waiting room—in 1892. The lavishly decorated waiting room had a mosaic floor, marble wainscoting and a ceiling of stuccowork. A large arched window of "cathedral glass set in rich and glowing colors" looked out onto Lake Michigan. Meeks regards the St. Louis and Chicago stations as marking the end of a great era in American station-building. One last important phase would follow, in which the railroads, in the full flood of their power and pride, would indulge in a veritable spree of monument-building—memorials, as it would prove, to an era and a way of life that even then had begun to pass from the scene.

Left: *The Gothic Revival depot at Point of Rocks, Maryland, opened about 1873 at the junction of the Baltimore & Ohio main line and the branch line to Washington, D.C. This photo dates from about 1930.*

Victorian Designs

The Canadian Pacific's generously dormered, broad-porched fieldstone passenger depot (opposite, above) was the pride of McAdam, New Brunswick, a railroad junction town some 40 miles southwest of Fredericton, the provincial capital. Its Chateauesque roof is adorned with decorative finials.

At left, the Central Railroad of New Jersey's brick passenger depot at Jim Thorpe, Pennsylvania, dating from 1888, featured a cylindrical three-story-tall tower among its Romanesque-style details. Rapunzel herself might have leaned out of one of the upper windows. The Central Railroad of New Jersey ran day trips to this Pocono Mountains resort beginning in 1891.

The Queen Anne-style depot shown above opened in Oakland (formerly Slab Town), Maryland, about 1885. It served vacationers on the Baltimore & Ohio Railroad bound for the mountains of western Maryland, billed as "the Switzerland of America."

Old Grand Central Depot, New York City *Above*
Shipping tycoon Cornelius Vanderbilt commissioned the first
Grand Central Depot in New York City, built in the Second
Empire style from 1869 to 1871. The Palace of the Louvre in
Paris and London's St. Pancras Station inspired architect
John B. Snook. The station could not accommodate the
growth in traffic in the late years of the nineteenth century;
it gave way to the magnificent 1913 building that stands in
its place today.

In Praise of Freight *Opposite*
This elaborate allegorical façade no doubt inspired the
warehousemen who wrestled with shipments by the boxcar-
load at the New York City freight depot of Commodore
Vanderbilt's Hudson River Railroad. Opened in 1870, the
building was located at Hudson and Varick Streets in the
Greenwich Village neighborhood. Its ornamental carved relief
panel depicts the golden age of ocean and steam-train cargo.

Port City Railroad Facilities

The railroad workshop (above), in Savannah, Georgia, dates from 1852. Savannah was a leading railroad center and seaport for cotton shipments to the United States in the decade leading up to the Civil War.

At left is the 1889 Central Railroad of New Jersey ferry and Railroad Terminal at Jersey City, designed by the renowened Boston-based architectural firm of Peabody and Stearns. Major additions to improve the ferry facilities were completed in 1914. This landmark terminal, which was built on reclaimed land, is today part of Liberty State Park and is the New Jersey ferry point for visitors to the Statue of Liberty.

Roundhouses

Workmen pose aboard a gleaming Illinois Central Railroad locomotive in front of the roundhouse shown opposite, above, at Centralia, Illinois. The photo dates from 1861. "Cabbage stack" locomotives stand idle in the yard in this 1871 photograph. Below, a new complex of roundhouse and shops rose from the ashes of the original Baltimore & Ohio yard at Martinsburg, West Virginia. Confederate troops badly damaged the B&O's Martinsburg works during the Civil War, and the buildings shown in this photograph were added over the following decade to expand the facility to 11 acres devoted to railroad use.

New England Victoriana *Below and Opposite*
The Queen Anne-style passenger depot at Chatham, Massachusetts (below), built in 1887, is today a railroad museum. Passenger and freight service to the Cape Cod town ended in the late 1930s. The junction Union Depot at Canaan, Connecticut (opposite), served thirty-six trains per day during the first decade of the twentieth century—twenty trains of the Central New England Railroad and sixteen of the New York, New Haven & Hartford. The 1872 building, with board-and-batten siding and a polygonal corner tower, served passengers for almost a century, closing only in 1971.

Masonry Angles and Arches *Overleaf*
The Canadian Pacific Railroad outgrew its station at Quebec City and moved to a neighboring depot, the elaborate Gothic-inspired turreted structure shown on page 47, top.

The Canadian Pacific opened Windsor Station in Montreal (page 46, below) in 1888. The four-story Richardsonian Romanesque-style stone station cost $250,000.

Square towers with Italianate cornices and rooflines gave the first Union Station at Spruce and Asylum streets in Hartford, Connecticut, the air of a fortress (page 47, below). A new Richardsonian Romanesque-style Union Station replaced this building in 1889.

The North American West

The frontier seemed illimitable in 1865. President Lincoln, a Westerner himself, and the newspaper editor Horace Greeley, famous for exhorting young men to go West, thought at least a century would pass before Americans would fully settle the Great Plains. The railroads changed all that. The rail network west of the Mississippi River totaled 900 miles in 1865, the year of Lincoln's death. By 1910 it covered 87,000 miles. In that span, the railroads transported hundreds of thousands of homesteaders to the once-trackless prairie that stretched from the Mississippi to the Rockies.

Visionaries had dreamed of a transcontinental line from the earliest days of railroading. Citizens of Dubuque, Iowa, called a public meeting to discuss a Pacific railway as early as 1836. The Western expeditions of John C. Frémont in the 1840s increased interest in such a project. Asa Whitney, a wealthy merchant who regarded the railroad as an essential component of the China trade, lobbied hard for it, presenting a detailed plan to Congress in 1844. The government sponsored a series of railroad surveys in the 1850s, but the North-South dispute over slavery and states' rights blocked a final decision on the route. The outbreak of the Civil War in 1861 deprived the South of its veto and broke the deadlock. With the Pacific Railway Act of July 1, 1862, the first of the North American transcontinental lines began to take form.

The act chartered the Union Pacific to build westward from Omaha, Nebraska, while the Central Pacific pushed east from Sacramento across the barrier of the Sierra Nevada to the California-Nevada line. This measure, and supplemental legislation, promised generous subsidies to both concerns in the form of land grants and government-backed loans. Engineering difficulties could be overcome, Union Army railroad builder Grenville Dodge (1831–1916) told President Lincoln in the spring of 1863, just a few weeks before the Battle of Gettysburg. As for assuming the burden of cost, that was another matter. Without government aid, no existing organization could attempt such a vast project.

"I said I thought it should be taken up and built by the government," Dodge recalled advising the president. "He objected to this, saying the government would give the project all possible aid and support, but could not build the road; that it had all it could possibly handle in the conflict now going on."

Opposite: *A tiled dome rises above the Santa Fe Railway's Spanish Mission-style station in San Diego, built in 1915.*

Below: *Railroads built passenger and freight traffic by offering inducements to migrants, as the broadside shows. The rides were free and the lands cheap and rich, promised the Kansas Pacific.*

With this assurance, the Union Pacific broke ground near Omaha, on the Missouri River frontier, late in 1863. The government supported the first transcontinental railroad line with $60 million in loans and grants of millions of acres of public lands—prairie and townsites the Union Pacific could sell to farmers and speculators. Just as importantly, the government's generous Homestead Act of 1862 spurred the westward migration essential to railroad profitability. The act offered 160 acres of public domain to a settler for a nominal fee. It stimulated passenger traffic westward in the form of migrants, and, in turn, freight traffic eastward in the form of grain shipments from the newly opened Great Plains wheatfields.

The line advanced fitfully at first. Grading crews began work in the fall of 1864, and the first rails were laid in July 1865. Momentum began to build after the Confederate collapse that year. In May 1866 Dodge took charge of the project as the Union Pacific's chief engineer. His fastidious predecessor, Peter Dey, had resigned in protest of Union Pacific management's stock manipulations and corrupt construction practices. Dodge had no such scruples. He meant to get the railroad built. Stocks, finances, UP's phantom contracting company, known as the Credit Mobilier—these were somebody else's concern.

The route ran roughly along the 42nd parallel, following the North Platte River (and the old Oregon Trail) for much of the distance. Survey parties fanned out ahead of the construction crews, usually twenty men, heavily armed, often under the command of a Union army ex-officer. The small, widely scattered regular army offered scant protection on the frontier, and the road builders suffered casualties from the start. The Plains tribes, not surprisingly, regarded the railroad as an encroachment. They feared, too, that their chief source of sustenance, the great buffalo herds, would be disturbed and, ultimately, dispersed.

Dodge pushed the forward construction camps ahead every few days. The grading crews could prepare about 100 miles of line per month on level ground. The bridge gangs usually operated 5 to 20 miles ahead of the crews that laid the ties and rails. The rail crews laid 1 to 3 miles of track per day, depending on terrain; one day they managed 8 ½ miles. Other work parties put up temporary shelters for materials, and wood and water storage stations for the trains that ferried supplies and laborers from the Missouri River beachhead. Forty cars were needed to haul the material necessary for a single mile of track. At the peak, Dodge had some 10,000 laborers and 10,000 draft animals on the job. By the end of 1866, the Union Pacific stretched to North Platte, Nebraska, some 293 miles west of Omaha.

The base camps, improvisational "hell on wheels" communities of saloonkeepers, prostitutes, gamblers and confidence men, advanced westward with the rails. When Robert Louis Stevenson passed through on a transcontinental journey in the late 1870s, he remarked upon "how at each stage of the construction, roaring impromptu cities, full of gold and lust and death, sprang up and then died away again, and are now but wayside stations in the desert." A few of the camps—North Platte; Julesburg, Colorado; Cheyenne, Wyoming—would develop into respectable towns, with the first permanent freight and passenger stations along the UP route.

Dodge's gangs completed 450 miles of line in 1867–68. Indian attacks were most frequent on the long Plains stretch between Fort Kearney, Nebraska, and Bitter Creek, Wyoming. In the summer of 1867, a Sioux war party attacked a Mormon grading crew near the site of Cheyenne, killing two men. They were buried in the first graveyard of Wyoming's future capital. Another war party captured and set fire to a train. Ranging far ahead of the construction gangs, surveyors were subject to routine harassment.

The elements conspired, too. The plan for 1868 called for the Union Pacific to build another 480 miles west to Salt Lake City, with the ultimate goal of meeting the east-building Central Pacific in 1869 at Humboldt Wells, another 200 miles down the line. By then the race was on, both railroads building at a furious pace. The financiers

put Union Pacific crews under tremendous pressure to advance so the road could collect the maximum in government land grants and bond subsidies. From the head office in New York came the directive to work through the cold season. "Winter caught us in the Wasatch Mountains," Dodge recalled, "but we kept on grading our road and laying our track in the snow and ice at a tremendous cost." He estimated the additional expense of the winter campaign at $10 million. By May 1, 1869, the railroad had reached Promontory, Utah, for a total of 534 miles of track laid over a period of twelve months.

The Union Pacific came abreast of and passed its fast-building rival from the West, and for a time the two roads were actually grading parallel lines. Four Sacramento merchants—grocer Leland Stanford, the hardware partners Collis P. Huntington and Mark Hopkins, and dry-goods dealer Charles Crocker—had gained control of the Central Pacific in 1862. The Big Four solved the California labor shortage by importing thousands of Chinese workers. After a slow start, the railroad breached the Sierra Nevada barrier and pushed eastward across the high plains of Nevada.

The Central Pacific reported less conflict with Western Native Americans than its rival encountered on the Plains. The Great Basin tribes were more widely scattered, less warlike than the hard-riding Sioux, and had no buffalo

herds to protect. Perhaps, too, the railroad practiced a more effective style of diplomacy than did the Union Pacific. "We gave the old chiefs a pass each, good on the passenger cars," Huntington recalled, "and we told our men to let the common Indians ride on the freight cars whenever they saw fit." Skirmishes did break out, however, between Central Pacific and Union Pacific construction crews. There were ambushes and dynamite attacks as the two lines furiously prepared roadbed side by side. The government stepped in finally, mediating a junction at Promontory Point, Utah, a few miles west of Ogden.

The two railroad companies arranged for eastbound and westbound specials to meet at Promontory on May 10, 1869. From the east came Thomas C. Durant, a Union Pacific vice-president, and lesser dignitaries. From the west came the Big Four, Stanford, Huntington, Hopkins and Crocker. On a bright, cold Monday, the tycoons took turns tapping in ceremonial silver and golden spikes. Durant and Stanford drove the last golden spike home with a silver sledge, and the engineers ran their locomotives up until they touched. Then the entire party retired to the cars for speechmaking and to tap the endless flow of celebratory champagne.

Thus the first transcontinental line was opened. The final tally showed 1,038 miles of Union Pacific line and 742 miles for the Central

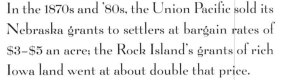

Pacific. As Dodge remembered it, trains were passing regularly in both directions within a day or two of the Golden Spike ceremony. Not long afterward, the Credit Mobilier scandal broke, and the reputations of a number of congressmen were permanently stained. But no one forfeited any gains. Historian John F. Stover estimates that the leading figures of the Union Pacific took $23 million in stocks, bonds and cash for themselves. The Big Four in California did nearly as well out of the Central Pacific.

Here was thievery on a grand scale. As Stover noted, though, it was in the spirit of the times—and at least the railroad builders *delivered*. "Even though their business ethics were low, the completed Pacific railroads were genuine accomplishments which hastened the economic expansion of the entire nation," he wrote. And the transcontinental lines accelerated the settlement of the frontier by generations. In the Dakotas alone, the population increased from 14,000 in 1870 to 500,000 in 1900.

New towns rose from the prairie along the lines of the west-building railroads. By 1871 the government had granted 170 million acres of public lands to some eighty railroad companies, most of them west of the Mississippi. In Montana, for example, the government assigned 15 percent of the territory's land to the railroads.

In the 1870s and '80s, the Union Pacific sold its Nebraska grants to settlers at bargain rates of $3–$5 an acre; the Rock Island's grants of rich Iowa land went at about double that price.

The railroads marketed their holdings aggressively, presenting the Great Plains as a farmers' Eden. Agents recruited in the eastern United States and in Europe. Railroad representatives often met prospective homesteaders at the ship: A special railroad depot opened for immigrants at Castle Garden in New York City. Railroad advertisements lured migrants with special fares and promises of cheap land of boundless fertility. Some lines arranged so-called Zulu cars for homesteaders—boxcars fitted out to transport settlers west with their families, household goods, farm equipment and livestock, all at a bargain rate. In Canada, special "colonist" cars carried homesteaders to the prairies, with their possessions following by freight.

As often as not, the first—and most important—buildings in the new towns were railroad depots. Railroads usually built the earliest Western stations to dimensions that would allow for transport from place to place on flatcars, for if one site failed to "take," another might succeed somewhere down the line. Stations for construction workers and homesteaders went up in such places as North Platte and Julesburg, temporary settlements that soon claimed permanent status. Services were minimal at first. The Union Pacific eventually introduced a standard design to replace first-generation shacks and abandoned boxcars lined with buffalo hides to keep out the winter blasts. These depots, sometimes landscaped, were the handsomest and most appealing structures in many raw, hastily knocked-together Plains or mountain towns.

The first Union Pacific station in Rawlins, Wyoming, opened in 1868. The railroad named the town for John Rawlins, General Ulysses S. Grant's consumptive wartime chief of staff, who had traveled along the construction route for his health as Dodge's guest in the summer of 1867. That first depot served the town of Rawlins, which became an important Union Pacific division point, until 1901.

Below: *Rival construction crews of the Union Pacific and the Central Pacific raise a champagne toast to celebrate the driving of the Golden Spike at Promontory, Utah, in May 1869. The ceremony marked the completion of the first transcontinental railroad.*

Early settlers dismissed Cheyenne's first depot as a "cowshed." The first trains stopped at Greeley, Colorado, in 1869, where a boxcar, a hotel and a log building served successively as the depot until a permanent stone station opened there in 1883. Union Pacific built the station at Hershey, Nebraska, 13 miles west of North Platte, to a standard design in 1892. It was a one-story wooden combination passenger and freight station, smartly tricked out in the exterior UP paint scheme of yellow and brown.

The Western building boom continued to the century's end. Land brought migrants; migrants settled the towns and dry-farmed tens of thousands of prairie acres. Congress approved the second transcontinental railroad, the Northern Pacific, in 1864, with the promise of a grant of 40 million acres of public lands. The charter authorized it to build from Lake Superior to a port in the Pacific Northwest. Construction gangs laid the first rails in Minnesota in February 1870. By 1873 the NP had completed 500 miles of track to the nascent town of Bismarck, North Dakota, which was named for Germany's "iron chancellor." The Sheridan House Hotel served as the depot there until 1901, when the Northern Pacific opened a handsome Spanish Mission-style station with a clay-tile roof and domed towers.

The Panic of 1873 and the subsequent depression stalled the line at Bismarck for several years. After a reorganization, new management under Henry Villard (1835–1900), a German-born one-time Civil War correspondent turned financier, pushed the line westward with a construction force that peaked at 25,000 men, half of them Chinese. The last rails were laid west of Helena, Montana, on September 8, 1883, and joined to Villard's Oregon Railway building from the west. The Northern Pacific eventually fulfilled its charter obligation by completing its own line to Seattle.

Like most large roads, the Northern Pacific developed a standard station design. For small, remote places, the railroad built a one-story frame building 18 feet by 46 feet, with an agent's dwelling attached. The depot had a board-and-batten exterior and a shingle roof. Inside were a waiting room, an office, a baggage room, two bedrooms and a kitchen.

The Headquarters Hotel in Billings, Montana, served as the Northern Pacific depot for more than twenty years after the first trains steamed into town in 1883. By 1909 Billings had become a rail hub, and the NP opened a new passenger station there to serve a flourishing traffic. The building, brick with sandstone trim, had Palladian windows and other Georgian Revival details. A separate baggage building stood to the east. The first NP station in Ellensburg, Washington, opened in 1886. A two-story frame structure, it gave way in 1910 to a brick depot in Spanish Colonial style. The railroad moved the original wooden building across the tracks, where it survived in industrial use into the 1990s.

Above: *"Skyscraper" dormitory cars followed railroad work gangs across the Great Plains. The soldiers riding the flatcar were detailed to protect workers from hostile action by Native Americans.*

Below: *The Burlington & Missouri Railroad advertises bargain-rate farmland for sale.*

The Northern Pacific depot in fast-growing Spokane, Washington, opened about 1886. The road's chief engineer, C.B. Talbot, designed a one-story complex with an exterior of upright and horizontal ornamental boarding. A 19-foot covered passageway connected two separate buildings, one for passenger services, the other designated for freight, baggage and the express and telegraph offices. An NP predecessor, the Seattle, Lake Shore and Eastern Railroad, opened a handsome depot at Snoqualmie, Washington, in 1889. A combination passenger and freight station of one-and-a-half stories, it had wooden cladding, an octagonal bay for the agent's office and a tower.

Through the sheer force of his will, Ontario-born tycoon James J. Hill (1838–1916) built the third transcontinental railroad, the Great Northern. Starting from small beginnings with the grandly named but moribund St. Paul & Pacific in Minnesota, in 1878 Hill moved first to extend the line north to Winnipeg, Manitoba, to connect there with the westward-building Canadian Pacific. Then he pushed west through North Dakota and into Montana. Hill's railroad reached Great Falls in 1887. Six years later, the first Great Northern train rolled into the line's western terminus at Seattle.

By then, the Canadian Pacific had reached the new town of Vancouver, British Columbia, in what railroad historian Stewart Holbrook has called "one of the great construction epics of North America." Chartered in February 1881, the CP opened the main line between Montreal and Vancouver only four-and-a-half years later. On Hill's recommendation, the railroad put Illinois-born William C. Van Horne in charge of construction in 1882. With work gangs numbering up to 10,000 men, Van Horne oversaw the extension of the line from Winnipeg across the prairie at the rate of 2 to 3 miles per day. At the same time, a subcontractor built eastward slowly from Vancouver.

In about a year, Van Horne's crews laid more than 500 miles of track, put up thirty-two stations—and reached the towering Rockies. The grading and track-laying gangs pushed on through the mountains in 1884 and 1885. Canadian Pacific grandees drove home the last spike at Cragellachie, 2,534 miles west of Montreal and 251 miles east of Vancouver, on November 11, 1885. At first, the CP used a wooden shed on the harborfront as its western terminus. A larger station, built in the grand French Chateau style with steeply pitched roofs and conical towers, soon replaced it.

Far to the south, two other transcontinental systems were completed in the 1880s. After Promontory Point in 1869, the Central Pacific's Big Four turned their attention southward. Building east from Los Angeles, the Southern Pacific reached Tucson, Arizona, in 1882 and

Right: This noble Neoclassical station in Vancouver, British Columbia, served the transcontinental trains of the Canadian Pacific Railroad.

Left: *The passenger depot at Raton, New Mexico, a Santa Fe Railroad division point, accommodated sixty trains per day when it opened in 1904. In this photograph, the Mission-style stucco station sleeps undisturbed in the midday sun.*

sent the first trains over the new transcontinental link in 1883, after a junction with the Texas & Pacific near El Paso, Texas. The Atchison, Topeka & Santa Fe developed slowly. Chartered in Kansas in 1859, the railroad won a 3-million-acre government land grant in 1863, but had only reached the Colorado line by 1872. The pace picked up thereafter, though, and by 1889 the Santa Fe operated 7,000 miles of route from Chicago south to the Gulf of Mexico and west to California.

The Santa Fe also gave Harvey House restaurants to the world. Robert Louis Stevenson had complained of halts for a few minutes at stations "with a meagre show of rolls and sandwiches for sale," and historical inquiry has confirmed that the author of *Dr. Jekyll and Mr. Hyde* had cause to disdain railroad fare. "In the 1870s the worst food served in the United States was unquestionably that put before travelers in the quick-lunch restaurants of depots," wrote Stewart Holbrook. "A whole literature and a comic art grew up around the quick-lunch, showing it as a madhouse where maniacal travelers fought each other for the privilege of buying ptomaine poisoning, at high prices, while at the door stood a stern, blue-coated railway conductor, watch

in hand, to hurry them to even greater bursts of gustatory speed." Then Frederick Henry Harvey changed all that.

A Londoner who emigrated to the United States about 1850, Harvey approached the Santa Fe in 1876 with a proposal to open an eating house in the station at Topeka, Kansas. The railroad scheduled an eating stop there, and Harvey supplied a good meal for a modest $1.00. Food, freshly starched linens and service were always top-quality. The notion caught on, and Harvey moved to expand. His advertisements sought "Young women of good character, attractive and intelligent, 18 to 30" to staff the restaurants. Harvey Girls lived in dormitories supervised by a matron, and had to observe a ten o'clock curfew. They received a starting wage of $17.50 a month, plus room, board and tips. In their standard attire of black dress with a white collar and black bow, black shoes and stockings, Harvey Girls became famous throughout the West. By 1901 Harvey and the Santa Fe operated fifteen hotels, forty-seven restaurants and thirty dining cars. Although many Harvey Houses closed during the Great Depression of the 1930s, the survivors were serving 30 million meals a year as late as 1943.

The restaurants are long gone today, except for one at an excursion-line depot in Hugo, Oklahoma, but Harvey hotel buildings survive in Santa Fe, New Mexico; Barstow, California; and a few other places. The 1880 Santa Fe station in Topeka no longer stands, nor does the first Union Pacific station there, which had been part of a three-story hotel built in 1872. From the 1880s through the 1920s, second-generation stations replaced the original depots all along the transcontinental lines.

Nebraska architect Thomas Kimball designed a Greek Revival station for the Chicago, Quincy & Burlington in Omaha in 1898. (A Chicago firm extensively altered the building in the late 1920s.) Kimball also designed a fine station for the Burlington at the important railroad center of Hastings, Nebraska. An early example of the Spanish Colonial-Revival style, the Hastings depot, opened in 1906, stood two stories high, with a light-colored brick exterior and a Spanish tile roof. Inside, the main waiting room had a white marble fountain and eight-foot-high marble wainscoting along the walls.

The architectural firm of Reed and Stem of St. Paul, Minnesota, drew up the plans for the Mission-style Northern Pacific depot in Bismarck, opened in 1901. Twin bell towers surmounted a stucco exterior and clay-tile roof.

Cherry trim and mosaic floors decorated the interior spaces, which included men's and women's waiting rooms and railroad offices. James J. Hill's Great Northern commissioned staff architect Samuel L. Bartlett to design a series of depots across North Dakota and Montana. The Fargo station, opened in 1906, featured an outsized four-faced clock tower rising from a sandstone structure. A green-tiled hipped roof extended to cover open pavilions at either end of the station.

The firm of Brunt and Howe designed Cheyenne, Wyoming's, new Union Pacific station of 1887 in the Richardsonian Romanesque style. The exterior was of red and gray Colorado sandstone; a slender 120-foot-tall clock tower rose high above the town. Inside were a separate waiting room and lunch counter for emigrants. The second-generation station down the line in Rawlins, constructed of red brick with granite trim, boasted a pagoda-shaped tower with Gothic detailing about the windows.

The Spanish style proliferated in the Southwest and California, especially in Atchison, Topeka & Santa Fe towns. The Santa Fe built a large Spanish Colonial-Revival depot in Amarillo, Texas, in 1910. It contained waiting rooms segregated by race and sex, and a Harvey House restaurant with a Harvey Girls dormitory on the second floor. Covered archways provided shelter from the fierce Texas sun. The Santa Fe's Mission-style depot at Fourth and Andy Devine Streets in Kingman, Arizona, a long, narrow building with a pebbled stucco exterior, opened in 1907, replacing a dilapidated two-story frame building and its predecessor, a boxcar. Inside, the agent's office separated the men's and ladies' waiting rooms. Kingman's Harvey House restaurant survived here until 1938.

As the West's major cities grew in the early twentieth century, so, too, did their railroad stations become larger and more extravagant. Houston's three-story, white-terra cotta Union Station opened in 1911 on an 18-acre site at a cost of more than $500,000. Denver's first Union Station, with a distinctive Victorian Gothic clock tower 180 feet tall, dated from 1881. The ground floor had a "sample room"—a bar. Large wings were added at either end in 1892. In 1915 a grandiose Beaux-Arts building replaced the original structure. In temperate San Diego, the Santa Fe's Mission-style depot, opened in 1915, featured a large, elaborate forecourt with arcades and an open-air waiting room.

The new Union Passenger Terminal in Los Angeles consumed decades in the planning: Site and style disputes delayed the project interminably, and the U.S. Supreme Court had to intervene before construction could start. The design, as finally approved, blended Spanish styles recalling the city's past with modernist Art Deco details. Mary Colter, Fred Harvey's architect/interior designer, decorated the restaurant, cocktail lounge, luncheonette, soda fountain and shops. Union Terminal opened in 1939 with a gaudy three-day celebration that drew an estimated 500,000 people. It was the last great American railroad station to open before World War II.

However, within a few years, the station's modern attractions would seem spurious. It fell into disuse, as auto and airplane travel burgeoned during the 1950s. Union Terminal gained a new lease on life in the 1990s, though, with the development of a subway and commuter rail system for greater Los Angeles. And most of the terminal's original features—including huge chandeliers, bronze-framed doorways and landscaped patios—survived the neglect of earlier decades to charm and awe a new generation of travelers.

Left: *Harvey Girls take a photo break in front of the station at Syracuse, Kansas. By 1901, Harvey Houses were serving good fare at reasonable prices at Syracuse and forty-six other Santa Fe Railroad stations.*

A Desert Landmark *Previous pages*
The Santa Fe Railroad opened the Casa del Desierto—
station, hotel and restaurant—in Barstow, California, in 1911.
The city bought and restored the magnificent old resort;
renovations were temporarily halted when an earthquake
damaged four of the Casa's towers in 1992.

California Hubs *Opposite, right and below*
An early automobile discharges travelers at the Santa Fe's La Grande Station in Los Angeles in the first years of the last century (opposite). The 1906 earthquake demolished the Southern Pacific Depot at Third and Townsend Streets in San Francisco. This view (below) from streetside shows the old depot circa 1890. A Mission-style station, later destroyed by human agency, replaced the rather homey structure. At right, the Train Board announces local and long-distance arrivals at the Southern Pacific's 1915 station.

A Narrow-Gauge Attraction *Below*
The clapboard depot at Durango, Colorado, opened
in 1881, served the Silverton branch of the narrow-gauge
Denver & Rio Grande Railroad, which runs through
the San Juan Mountains.

Silver Mining's Legacy *Above*

The 1882 station at Silverton, Colorado, 45 miles north of Durango, was the northern terminus of a branch of the Denver & Rio Grande Railroad, originally built to transport workers and ore during the silver-mining boom of the nineteenth century. The station's restorers repainted the building in the Rio Grande's tan and brown livery during the 1970s. Today, coal-powered steam trains operate along this popular scenic excursion route for tourists from around the world.

Union Pacific Depots

The substantially built brick depot of Dillon, Montana (opposite, above), opened in 1909. The role of the railroad in its history is evidenced by the fact the president of the Union Pacific Railroad bequeathed his name to the town.

Passengers and crew pose in front of the "Payne Special" (left) at rest in Keystone, Nebraska. Above, a grain elevator towers above the depot of the Great Plains town of Madison, Nebraska. Railroads relied on grain shipments to generate profits on their long Western routes through sparsely settled country.

Faces of the West

A four-faced clock tower surmounts the eclectic brick station at Helena, Montana (left). Below, a dining car is fancifully built into the street side of a passenger depot at Saskatoon, Saskatchewan.

The arrowlike clock tower of the station at Great Falls, Montana (opposite), advertised the Chicago, Milwaukee & St. Paul Railroad in mosaic tiles on all four sides. The "Milwaukee Road," as it was popularly known, abandoned the station in the late 1950s, when it was sold into private hands.

Passenger Depo

The Glory Days

The Union Pacific's Richardsonian Romanesque station in Cheyenne, Wyoming (opposite, above), opened in 1887 with a cathedral-style clock spire that soared 120 feet high. Opposite, below, the legend atop the 150-foot-tall clock tower at the Portland, Oregon, Union Station, installed in 1948, exhorts travelers to choose the rails over private automobiles and airlines. Amtrak still uses the waiting room.

Young men of Phoenix, Arizona, demonstrate an alternate form of transportation in front of one of the city's two depots dating from the Territorial era (above). Arizona became a state in 1912. At right, this photograph of the station at Winnipeg, Manitoba, dates from 1899. By then, the Canadian Pacific had been operating regular service between the growing Red River city and Montreal for fourteen years.

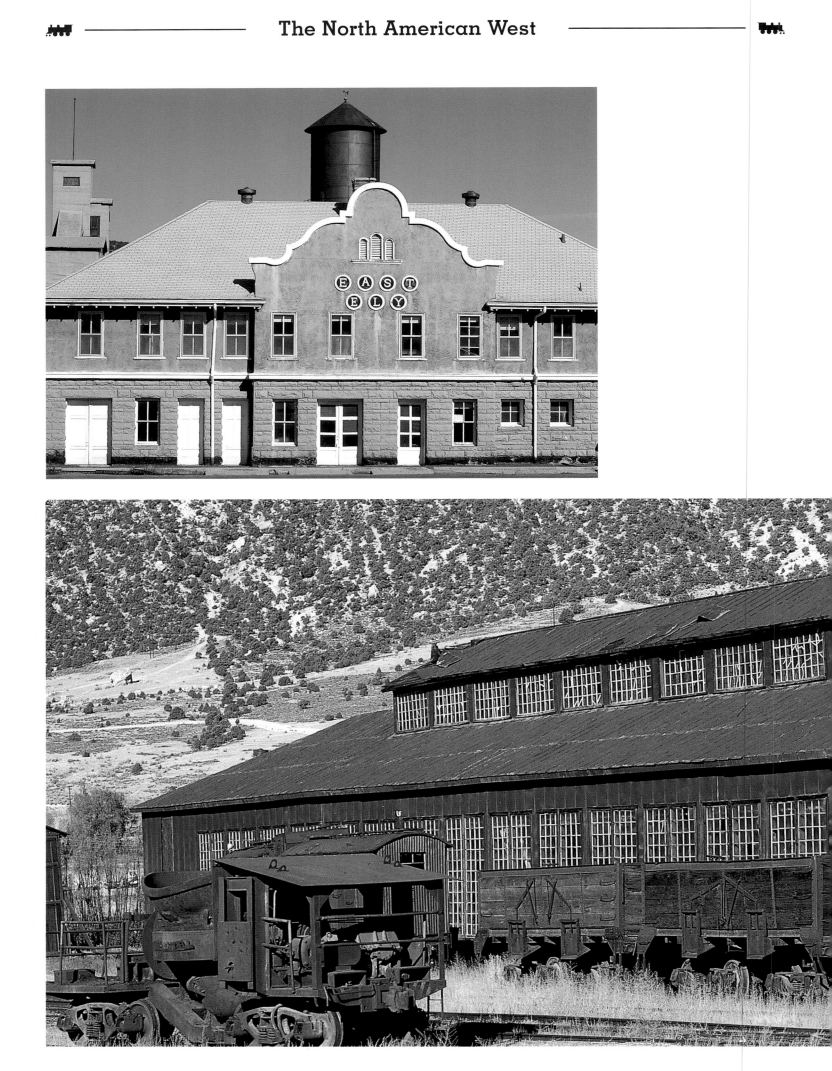

Preserved Buildings at East Ely, Nevada

The Nevada Northern Railroad made its headquarters in
the East Ely, Nevada, depot, opened in 1907. The station and
adjacent buildings are today part of a railroad museum.
The copper-ore-carrying Nevada Northern Railroad used
the freight buildings at the East Ely station, shown at
left and above, while passengers and office staff were
accommodated in the stone-clad and stucco-faced building
seen opposite, above.

Santa Fe Landmarks

Architect Mary E.J. Colter designed the blockhouse-like
Navajo Hotel in Gallup, New Mexico (above), an important
stop on the Santa Fe Railroad. Colter, influenced by the
ideas of the American Arts and Crafts Movement, worked
extensively for the Santa Fe Railway and Fred Harvey
Company. Her work includes three buildings on the South
Rim of the Grand Canyon National Park: Hopi House;
Lookout Studio; and Bright Angel Lodge.

The Santa Fe station at Dodge City, Kansas (opposite,
above), featured a Harvey House lunchroom, whose
trackside entry beckons just to the left of the platform
canopy. Shaded archways screened sun-shy passengers at
the Santa Fe depot in Amarillo, Texas (right). The Spanish
Colonial Revival building dates from 1910. The second floor
of the depot housed Santa Fe railroad offices and a Harvey
Girls dormitory.

The Mission Style *Previous pages and below*
The imposing Mission-style depot at Caliente, Nevada—
seen below and on the previous pages—opened in 1923.
Designed by John and Donald Parkinson of Los Angeles, the
Union Pacific station accommodated two restaurants and a
hotel. The Nevada town was a Union Pacific division point
and maintenance center for the railroad's steam locomotives
until 1948, when the UP's Nevada facilities were relocated to
Las Vegas. Today the handsomely restored depot building
serves as Caliente's City Hall.

Phoenix Union Station *Above*
The Southern Pacific depot at First and Jackson Streets
in Phoenix, Arizona (see page 69), survived until the early
1920s, when it made way for a new Mission-style Union
station designed by architect W.H. Mohr. The detail above
of the eastern façade shows the large open-sided waiting
room for passengers.

Northern Exposure *Above*
The subarctic sun throws the neat clapboard depot at Carcross, Yukon Territory, into sharp relief. The station served the White Pass and Yukon Railroad that traversed this sparsely settled region.

Wayside Sentinel *Below*
An angry sky overshadows the simple wooden Amador Central depot at Martell, California. Note the agent's bay window overlooking the tracks and the weathered siding on the gable end.

Scenes from the Steam Era

At right, the low wooden station at Lethbridge, Alberta, at the foot of the Canadian Rockies, housed waiting and baggage rooms and an agent's office. Below, passengers prepare to board a Canadian Pacific Railway train in this 1920s scene at Revelstoke, British Columbia, on the western flank of the Rockies. Opposite, below, this collector's item marks the arrival of the first passenger train at the Northern Pacific station in Minnewaukon, South Dakota, on August 1, 1885.

Rail Freight *Below*

A diesel locomotive pulls a containerized freight train slowly
past the abandoned and disintegrating depot at Winterhaven,
California. Before the emergence of the automobile,
California was built rapidly with the railroads, which
provided transportation not only for passengers, but freight
of all kinds, from heavy industrial goods to the perishable
fruits and vegetables so readily farmed in the Golden State.

A Forgotten Roundhouse *Above*

The ruins of a solidly built stone roundhouse are set against a Colorado mountain backdrop in this elegy to the railroad age. A steam boiler rusts away in the right foreground of the photograph. A network of narrow-gauge railroads provided the infrastructure for Colorado's nineteenth-century mining booms, many of whose impressive landmarks were long since abandoned to the elements.

Engine Houses

Opposite, above, railroad workers pose proudly next to Engines number 50 and 132 in front of the St. Louis & San Francisco Railroad's engine house at Anthony, Kansas, in 1890.

Vast stretches of North American forest were felled to power the first generations of steam locomotives. By the 1860s, railroads were turning increasingly to coal for fuel. "Betsey," a Cascade Railroad engine (right), emerges from her clapboard lair on the north bank of the Columbia River in the Washington Territory in 1867. Below, workers prepare to move the woodburner "Stowe" on a roundtable in an El Paso, Texas, railroad yard. From the 1880s, El Paso, on the Mexican border, was an important international rail center.

Small Towns, Suburbs and Resorts

From the vantage of the new century, it's hard to imagine how commanding a place the depot once held in rural and small-town life. Arrival and leave-taking ceremonies were enacted there, daily business transacted with the freight and telegraph offices, gossip exchanged, news gathered, mail collected and sent. In very small places, the station housed the post office and general store as well as passenger services. From the 1840s through the first decades of the twentieth century, railroad stations reigned unchallenged as the most important buildings in hundreds of American and Canadian towns.

"They were a kind of social center, the source of local news and gossip," Edwin P. Alexander wrote in his pictorial history *Down at the Depot*. "No one arriving or departing, stranger or resident, went unnoticed, and farewells and welcomes were sincere. In the days of the horse and buggy, the station was the only means of intercourse with the outside world."

Small-town and country halts were as diverse in style and mood as the localities they served. Large railroads mass-produced hundreds of stations to standard designs, but as time passed even pattern-built depots decorated in a road's livery—painted red and yellow-gold, say, for the Illinois Central—acquired a hometown patina. Standard ground plans usually placed a baggage room at one end and a waiting room at the other, with the agent's office in the middle. For all the kinship to stations down the line, though, the depot in Crawford, Georgia (1848), or

Mineral Point, Wisconsin (1857), spoke in the accents and cadences of home.

Comparatively few small-town depots survive from the nineteenth century, and fewer still are used for their original purpose. Railroads began contracting rural and branch-line services as early as 1910. The New York Central system alone operated 235 passenger stations in New York State in 1934; a quarter-century later, only 115 remained in service. Before World War I, 1,500 railroad and interurban stations were in use in Indiana. By the late 1980s, only 300 still stood, and only fifteen of those remained in railroad service.

What dramas, real and fictional, were enacted in these mostly vanished small-town depots! Young men went off to war by train in 1861 and 1898 and 1917 (1914 in Canada). Ringgold station, on the Western & Atlantic Railroad in north Georgia, built in 1850, went down in Civil War annals as the last station through which the Andrews raiders passed in the hijacked Confederate train the "General" on April 12, 1862. James A. Andrews and his band of Union saboteurs captured the train near Big Shanty (now Kennesaw), Georgia, with the aim of piloting it north and destroying track, telegraph lines and bridges behind them. The "General" ran out of water and wood just beyond Ringgold. Pursuing Confederates captured all twenty-two Yankees, and hanged Andrews and seven others a few weeks later.

Sherman's army turned up at Ringgold eighteen months later. The depot's thick sandstone walls proved sturdy enough to withstand a pow-

Opposite: *Smoke rises from the chimney of the meticulously maintained cobblestone station of snowclad Kensington, Prince Edward Island, Canada.*

Above: *With a rack riding proudly atop the headlamp, a McQueen locomotive built in Schenectady, New York, in 1868 pauses at the waystop of Little Laramie River, 15 miles west of Laramie, Wyoming.*

erful explosion during a battle for the town on November 27, 1863. The Western & Atlantic hastily patched the damaged corner of the Ringgold station with limestone blocks—a rough-and-ready repair that remained plainly visible for more than a century.

Country girls struck out for the city from village depots and flagstops innumerable. The novelist Theodore Dreiser's Carrie Meeber boarded the afternoon train for Chicago in August 1889, leaving the "familiar green environs" of her girlhood forever. "To be sure there was always the next station, where one might descend and return," mused the narrator of *Sister Carrie*. "There was the great city, bound up more closely by these very trains which came up daily. Columbia City was not so very far away, even once she was in Chicago." Carrie met a "drummer" in the train—a nineteenth-century archetype who proved her undoing. Traveling salesmen akin to Dreiser's Charles Drouet, along with the sharps and confidence men who journeyed with them in the smoker, stepped off the train into hundreds of small American and Canadian depots every day.

Traveling shows, lyceum lecturers, evangelists and faith healers arrived in small-town North America by train. Every four years offered the prospect of a whistlestop visit from a presidential campaigner, a whiff of the great world of political power and authority beyond the village limits. The railroad, as Abraham Lincoln observed, allowed a politician to "to see and be seen." In the summer and autumn of 1896, Democratic presidential candidate William Jennings Bryan made 569 speeches during his epic whistlestop campaign, traveling about the United States in a private Chesapeake & Ohio car. Eight years later, Republican Theodore Roosevelt covered 21,209 campaign miles by rail.

There was drama, too, in the ebb and flow of everyday life in even the smallest flagstops. Historian Stewart Holbrook gives the biography of the hamlet of Columbia Bridge, New Hampshire, in his book *The Story of American Railroads* (1947). The little depot, built in 1896 and named for the covered bridge that crossed the upper Connecticut River to Lemington, Vermont, served two Boston & Maine trains daily each way, north and south. The one-and-a-half story station had a 60-foot-long platform, a big stove in the center of the room and a privy out back, and it also housed the Columbia Bridge post office and Will Bailey's general store. Along with stocks of woolen clothing, patent medicine, candy and staple foods, the store had a slot machine and "a huge Swiss music box" for the entertainment of passengers and for that much more numerous group of depot regulars, loafers and loungers.

Boston & Maine trains calling at Columbia Bridge during the early years of the last century were basic: engine and tender, baggage car, smoker and day coach. When a passenger or two appeared, Will Bailey, who doubled as station agent, fitted the signal flag into its metal socket on the platform. The trains, rarely on time, announced themselves with a blast of the steam whistle, the cue for an explosion of activity in Columbia Bridge.

"I don't think I ever knew a railroad station that could change so quickly and so manifestly from deep calm, almost somnolence, to a state of excitement bordering on frenzy," wrote Holbrook. "The magic of the steam cars was never more apparent than here."

Railroad engineer Walter G. Berg, in his book *Buildings and Structures of American Railroads* (1892), supplied a precise definition of the Columbia Bridge type of depot: "stations of minor importance at which only a limited number of trains stop—usually on flags; hence the name." The simplest flag depot was an open or covered platform alongside the tracks. For a slightly busier halt, the railroad might enclose the platform on three sides, with the open side facing the track. In places with cold winters, the road often provided a one-room frame building looked after by the track foreman for that section of the line, a functionary "who keeps the place clean and sees that the door is unlocked during the day or at train time."

Depots in towns large enough to warrant an agent were usually indistinguishable in practice from the next category up, the local passenger depot, and they could be quite substantial, even distinguished, buildings. Henry Hobson Richardson, the leading American architect of his time, designed flag depots for the Boston & Albany Railroad at suburban Woodland, Waban, and Wellesley, Massachusetts. Woodland Station, near Boston, which opened shortly after Richardson's death in 1886, measured 36 feet by 16 feet. A single-story stone building with heavy, sloping roofs, it had a waiting room, a baggage room, men's and ladies' toilets and a ticket office.

At many local stations, the railroad housed passenger and freight services together in one building. In the standard layout of these "combination" stations, the office faced the track, with a bay window giving the agent an unobstructed view. There were waiting rooms for passengers, a baggage room, toilets, sometimes a separate express and mail room, living quarters for the station agent and his family, and a freight room.

The Minnesota & Northwestern Railroad's standard combination depot, designed in 1887, featured slight variations for different locales and conditions, according to Berg. But all were one-story frame structures with weatherboard sheathing, shingle roofs and a low platform on all four sides. Chesapeake & Ohio carpenters built the board-and-batten Alderson, West Virginia, station to a standard pattern in 1896. It had an agent's bay window facing the tracks and, in keeping with practice in the rigidly segregated South, separate waiting rooms for whites and blacks. By 1910 the C&O had used the design for more than 100 stations.

The Georgia Railroad retained prominent architect Bradford L. Gilbert to design the combination freight and passenger station at Grovetown, Georgia. Opened about 1890, the building measured 77 feet by 24 feet, with an exterior of cypress shingles stained with creosote and a metallic shingled roof. The station's most striking feature, a windmill turret, served as a waiting room for ladies; there were separate accommodations for whites and blacks. A large platform for handling cotton shipments ran alongside the freight room.

"The Grovetown station combines all these special features in a single, picturesque, and quaint building—one which helps the town, and that advertises and builds up the railroad as well," the *Railroad Gazette* noted with approval in September 1891.

By definition, local passenger depots provided passenger services only, according to Berg, with freight operations handled in a separate building. Like flagstops, these depots varied widely in size and amenities, depending on the importance of a place. The largest had a full suite of waiting rooms, baggage rooms, railroad offices, telegraph offices, mailrooms, dining rooms and newsstands. The Louisville & Nashville standard design had men's and ladies' waiting rooms and a smaller waiting room for blacks, as well as a ticket office and baggage rooms. The single-story L&N depot at Columbia, Kentucky, measured 20 feet by 90 feet. Along with the

Below: *Two travelers, alone, young and younger, await a Canadian Pacific Railroad train at somnolent Vermillion Bay, Ontario, in 1900.*

standard accommodations, the Columbia station had a restaurant and an office for the railroad's track department.

Richardson designed the junction station at Palmer, Massachusetts, to fit into the acute angle formed where the Boston & Albany and Central Vermont Railroads crossed. Opened in 1884, the granite structure had rounded arches and other Richardsonian flourishes, with a hipped roof that extended to form dormered porches on all four sides. Inside were a two-story waiting room, a dining room, a telegraph office, a shared ticket booth and separate agents' rooms for the two railroads.

Berg argued vigorously for functionality over ornamentation, perhaps in reaction to the gingerbread extravaganzas of the 1860s and '70s and the widespread popularity of Richardson's Romanesque Revival designs of the 1880s. He may well have been thinking of Richardson and his successors when he warned station designers against permitting aesthetic values to trump sound engineering standards:

"Much stress has been laid within recent years on providing artistic and picturesque structures for local passenger depots, especially at suburban points where the travel consists largely of wealthy patrons of the line," Berg wrote. That might be all right for very small stations with light traffic. But sacrificing conveniences of layout in larger depots courted disaster. He added, "It can hardly be considered good practice to design a large depot on the same outlines as a church or an old-fashioned country tavern, especially when very serious defects of the groundplan are created by giving too much attention to the architectural effect of the building."

Berg cited a Richardson flagstop along the Boston & Albany line at Chestnut Hill, Boston, as an example. A one-story granite building with limestone trim and a red-tile roof, it featured a large porte-cochère along the full length of the rear of the building. Heavy granite arches spanned the driveway. Inside were a general waiting room, a ladies' waiting room, a small baggage room and a small ticket office. "From an architectural and artistic standpoint this

design is most praiseworthy," Berg allowed, "but from a railroad engineer's standpoint there are serious defects in the ground plan." The water closet opened from the general waiting room, a "very objectionable" feature, he wrote, and the ticket office was "hardly large enough to warrant being called an office."

Most of Richardson's depot designs were for suburban places. Developers sited his Woodland Station, mentioned above, in an empty quarter of Newton, Massachusetts, with the specific purpose of attracting new householders who would take the train to their jobs in Boston. Thus Woodland Station played its small role in a mass shift of population from city to suburb underway in the United States in the last decades of the nineteenth century. Between 1850 and 1920, some 15 percent of the U.S. population moved to the suburbs in the so-called metropolitan corridors along railroad lines radiating outward from Eastern and Midwestern cities.

The Central Railroad of New Jersey operated commuter trains into and out of New York City at morning and evening rush hour as early as 1870. Railroads created the opportunity for growth outside the city center, and land developers seized it. Often, the first public building to go up in a new suburb was the railroad station. Leading citizens of these comfortable, quiet and leafy bedroom communities took great pride in their railroad.

"Viewing them as extensions of their elegant suburban homes and wanting to impress guests arriving by train, wealthy suburbanites sometimes distributed personal funds to build depots of sufficient distinction," Janet Greenstein Potter wrote in *Great American Railroad Stations* (1996). "Today, even without their former lawns, these small but architecturally sophisticated stations are among the earliest and best-preserved passenger stations."

As with larger stations, suburban depots varied widely in size and style. Edwin Alexander calls the little 1890s stone depot at Bycot, Pennsylvania, "probably the smallest station ever built." It served a changing section of Bucks County—farming, with some long-range commuting to Philadelphia. The station at Chestnut Hill, Pennsylvania, dating from the 1880s, formed part of a complex of buildings, including a five-stall roundhouse, a coaling dock and a water tank. The passenger station would survive the electrification of the line in the 1930s, though not the ancillary structures, purpose-built for steam. The Delaware, Lackawanna & Western set its station for the wealthy suburb of Morristown, New Jersey, in parklike grounds, with an approach that suggested entry into an opulent country estate. The depot itself, built of brick and limestone, drew on Renaissance Revival styles.

Railroads made once-remote wilderness areas accessible to a growing middle class with the money and leisure to travel. The cars brought thousands of excursionists to Down East and interior Maine; the White Mountains of New Hampshire; the mountain regions of western Maryland, West Virginia, North Carolina and Tennessee; and the great American and Canadian West.

Boston architect Nathaniel J. Bradlee designed the North Conway, New Hampshire, station, a White Mountains gateway that opened in 1874, in a style said to derive from Russian Provincial. Twin rectangular towers flanked a dormer with a clock. Horse-drawn equipages lined up under a broad platform to board passengers for the short trip to the area's upland hotels. The depot at nearby Bethlehem, built in a forest glade, claimed, according to the Pennsylvania Railroad, "the proud distinction of being the highest village east of the Rockies," at 1,450 feet above sea level.

At the Bangor & Aroostook's Greenville Junction station (1890), on the shore of Maine's Moosehead Lake, passengers stepped off the cars and into steamers bound for lakefront resorts. The Kent, Connecticut, station (1872), lay along the route to the Berkshires of Massachusetts, a popular summer destination for New York City vacationers. As late as the 1930s, eight trains a day stopped in Kent. The little station at Monteagle, Tennessee, on the Tracy City branch line of the Nashville,

Chattanooga & St. Louis, served the mountain resorts northwest of Chattanooga into the early years of the twentieth century. On the far side of the tracks, opposite the little station, stood a large water tank with an elaborately decorated rim. New York architect John H. Stem designed the Monon depot at French Lick, Indiana (1907), a hill spa famous for its mineral springs. The depot, with portes-cochère at either end and sidings for Pullman cars, was built of limestone that was quarried along the Monon line in Bedford, not far distant.

The railroads opened the West for tourists as surely as for homesteaders. By the first years of the twentieth century, excursion trains were running regularly to the California spas at Shasta Springs and Calistoga. The Union Pacific introduced through service to Yellowstone National Park in 1908. The UP built the original depot at West Yellowstone, Montana, of concrete, with trim in lava rock carved from the railroad right-of-way. A dining lodge and a dormitory for tourists were added later.

In the American Southwest, Harvey House restaurants at Santa Fe station stops offered Indian blankets and other souvenirs for sale to tourists passing through. Native American dance troupes performed for tour groups bound for the Western national parks or California. Indian artisans sometimes incorporated train motifs into the blankets displayed for sale. At least one rug had the legend "Fred Harvey" woven into it.

Above: *The station at the Adirondack Mountain resort of Lake Placid, New York, built to open the region to logging and tourism, is today an historical society museum.*

Mountain Resorts

Buses line up to ferry passengers to and from the Canadian Pacific station at the Rocky Mountain resort town of Banff, Alberta (opposite), in this photo from the summer of 1948. In the foreground, a couple admires the torpedolike form of the CP's Engine 5924.

Union Pacific passengers bound for the mining town of Park City, Utah, used this Queen Anne-style station (right) built in 1886 with its roof steeply pitched to shed mountain snows. Though the tracks of the narrow-gauge Echo & Park City Railroad are gone, private owners restored the depot in the early 1990s. Below, a Canadian Pacific train discharges passengers at the resort of Glacier House, British Columbia, in a photograph dating from about 1890.

Vacation Attractions *Above*

The Santa Fe Railroad opened this rustic log depot in 1910 for passengers bound for the South Rim of the Grand Canyon in Arizona. The railroad also built a luxury hotel, El Tovar, and other amenities designed to attract excursion travelers and thus boost business on its long-distance lines. The station is today a stop on an excursion railroad and a National Park Service office.

A Rustic Frame Station *Opposite*

This prosaic halt, now defunct, once hummed with the activity of passengers arriving and departing Fraser, British Columbia. Despite the demise of the railroad, as evidenced by the overgrown trackbed, the building retains its simple charm.

Connecticut Country Halts *Above and left*
The unhurried trains of the Valley Railroad called at the prim board-and-batten depot in the lower Connecticut River valley town of Chester, Connecticut (above). At left, the depot at Cornwall Bridge, in northwestern Connecticut, opened in 1886 on the line of the Housatonic Railroad, part of the New York, New Haven & Hartford. Five well-dressed gentlemen await the train's arrival in the shade of the overhanging eaves.

Architectural Expressions *Above and below*
The fanciful East Hartford stop of the New York & New England Railroad is pictured here in a quiet moment between trains in June 1928. Paying little heed to function, the architect added a Stick-style turret to the otherwise humble suburban halt. The dignified Arts-and-Crafts-inspired stone station (below), all dormers and projecting eaves, served Union Pacific patrons in Ontario, Oklahoma.

Victorian Detailing *Opposite*
The well-kept depot at Crawford's Notch, in New
Hampshire's White Mountain region, boasts Victorian
shingling, a corner turret and elaborate cornice work
among its period features.

From Ore to Tourists *Above*
The legendary Comstock Lode built the Virginia &
Truckee Railroad depot in Gold Hill, Nevada, opened
in 1872. The railroad once hauled silver ore from the
seemingly inexhaustible lode; the station is now a stop
on a tourist railroad.

A "Witches' Cap" Turret *Opposite*
A caplike shingled flared turret projects above the passenger depot at New Hope, Bucks County, Pennsylvania, on the Philadelphia & Reading Railroad. Philadelphia-bound commuters used the station; it later became a stop on a tourist railroad. George Washington made his famous crossing of the Delaware near New Hope.

The New Jersey Shore *Above*
This well-kept little station at Cold Spring, just north of the resort town of Cape May, recalls Cold Spring's role as a Victorian-era vacation spot for world-weary New Yorkers.

Branch-line Passenger Depot *Below*

The passenger halt at the Wilton, Connecticut, village of Cannondale is still in use as a stop for New York City commuters on Metro North's single-track South Norwalk–Danbury branch line. No longer a building in railroad service, however, the former station now houses a store. Commuters must buy their tickets and seek shelter from the elements elsewhere.

Elegant Fans and Gables *Above*

When the farmers and dairymen of the village of Compton, Quebec, just north of the Vermont border, needed to get to the market town of Sherbrooke for business or pleasure they began their journey here, at Compton's turreted and gabled railroad station.

Modest Suburban Depots

Designers of the Chicago & Northwestern commuter depot at Lake Forest, Illinois (above), worked in a Tudor Revival style, complete with a half-timbered gable. Preservation volunteers restored the building, opened about 1899, in the 1980s.

A handcart awaits its operator on a quiet day at the small combination passenger-freight depot of the north country village of Mercer, Wisconsin (opposite, above). At right, the lonely stone station at Tring Junction, Quebec, warms to the thaw; snowmelt forms puddles in front of the porte-cochère of the station. The junction lies 30 miles southeast of Quebec City, the provincial capital.

A Makeshift Solution *Below*
The elongated combination station at remote Gander,
Newfoundland, has a temporary look, as though waiting
to be hoisted upon the tracks for delivery to another town
farther up the line.

A Simple Waystop *Above*

A steam locomotive pulling a train of freight cars eases into
McEwen Station, a stop on the Sumpter Valley Railroad in
the arid, sparsely settled northeastern corner of Oregon.
Facilities in such remote stations as this one were scant, but
passengers could at least find shelter here, unlike the flagstops.
In the background of this scenic landscape, the Blue
Mountains rise abruptly from the stony plain.

A Whistlestop Preserved *Above*
Carpenter Gothic details ornament this 1877 depot at
Farmers Branch, Texas, once a small hamlet 11 miles
northwest of downtown Dallas and today a historic
preservation district nestled among the suburbs of the
Texas metropolis.

Benign Neglect *Below*
The modest woodframe way station at Cherry Hill, a farming region of Lancaster County, Pennsylvania, served a fluctuating, if small, population. Engine No. 90 moves past with a tender brimful of coal.

Ghost Town *Above*

The briefly busy Mission-style station in the flash-in-the-pan mining region of Rhyolite, Nevada, crumbles slowly under a high, bright sky. Once the center of the Bullfrog Mining District on the edge of Death Valley, Rhyolite today is as ghostly as the 1908 depot that bears its name.

Abandoned Halts *Opposite*

Grass-grown tracks lead faintly away from the bucolic station at Rock Island, Quebec, near the Vermont border (opposite, above). Below, rails rust and stringers rot in front of the cobblestone depot of Alberton, a fishing port near the northern tip of Prince Edward Island.

The Twentieth Century

In terms of the continent's municipal buildings, the early twentieth century was ushered in by the World's Columbian Exposition in Chicago. Organized to celebrate the 400th anniversary of Columbus's New World landfall, it ran from May to November 1893, set in a 150-building "White City" along the Lake Michigan shorefront. The world fair's buildings, designed under the general supervision of architect Daniel H. Burnham, were mainly Neoclassical and Renaissance in style—all triumphal arches, colonnades and vaulted and domed interiors. Burnham's work marked a turning point. For the next generation or so, great American public buildings, including railroad stations, would derive from the model of Chicago's White City.

With railroads reaching the peak of their power at the close of the nineteenth century, the great lines turned naturally to the monumental Beaux-Arts style. At the same time, the United States had attained status as a world economic and political force. The Neoclassical fashion in station design thus reflected both "a new national conceit and the megalomania of American railroad companies," in the words of Jeffrey Richards and John M. MacKenzie in *The Railway Station: A Social History.*

The historian Carroll Meeks put the matter even more bluntly: "Elephantiasis took over every aspect of railroading, including the terminals, now built to dimensions never before approached," he wrote in *The Railroad Station: An Architectural History.* "Such opulent dimensions were not func-

tionally necessary; the companies could afford magnificence and enjoyed their munificent role, as princes had in predemocratic ages."

So, just before the fall, American cities raised the greatest of monuments to the steam age. The design for the temporary station built for visitors to the Chicago world's fair set the tone. In Meeks's description, the building "had three deeply recessed arched portals, with engaged Corinthian columns framing the arches; towers surmounted by obelisks rose at the corners." Roman baths inspired the interior. More than 100,000 people a day used the depot, but its influence extended far beyond the six-month life of the fair. Railroads and their architects regarded Burnham's work as "the archetype of future stations." It introduced the Beaux-Arts mode, the last significant style of railroad architecture, and inspired grand terminal buildings in Boston, New York, Washington, D.C., Kansas City, New Orleans, Detroit and Toronto.

Opposite: *This detail shows the elaborate cornice of the Renaissance-style Reading Terminal in Philadelphia. The eight-story station opened in 1893.*

Below: *The Neoclassical styles of the White City at the 1893 World's Columbian Exposition in Chicago set the fashion for great American public buildings in the first decades of the twentieth century.*

Above: *A 663-foot-long Beaux-Arts masterpiece, Washington's Union Station opened in 1907. It's now a preservation success story, a restored monument with its original transportation function intact and new uses added as well.*

Right: *A detail of the Corinthian columns flanking the great arcaded entrance to the capital's Union Station.*

The greatest of all were two New York City monuments, Grand Central Terminal (1903–13) and Pennsylvania Station (1906–10), and Union Station in Washington, D.C. (opened in 1907). Vanderbilt's railroad empire had long since outgrown the first Grand Central of 1871, but it was a terrible train wreck in a tunnel leading into the station that spurred the new construction. A New York Central express and a commuter train collided in the smoke-filled Park Avenue tunnel, killing seventeen passengers and crewmen. Post-disaster legislation mandated the electrification of lines leading into Grand Central, and set the engineers and architects to thinking and planning in new ways.

Meeks called the result "one of the outstandingly successful stations of history." Built on multiple levels, the new Grand Central dealt smoothly with complex circulation problems, placing express trains above and commuter trains below, "each set of tracks being provided with a concourse of its own, so that in effect two stations are superimposed." The architects Reed and Stem of St. Paul, Minnesota, designed an extensive system of ramps to move as many as 110,000 passengers a day to and from the forty-eight platforms and in and out of the station. New York City architects Warren & Wetmore collaborated on the landmark structure.

An ornate sculpture group featuring a statue of Mercury topped Grand Central's Beaux-Arts façade. Inside, the main concourse stretched for 375 feet. A stunning blue-and-gold zodiac along the curved ceiling depicted 2,500 stars of the Mediterranean sky in winter. One sharp-eyed observer complained that the painter had transposed the stars west to east. "The ceiling is purely decorative," the railroad responded haughtily. "It was never intended that a mariner should set his course by the stars at Grand Central." More than 150,000 people toured the new building on opening day in 1913.

Architect Charles F. McKim supervised the design of Pennsylvania Station. A tunnel under the Hudson led to the underground recesses of the building on 32nd Street between Seventh and Eighth Avenues. For the façade, in pink- and beige-toned masonry, McKim found inspiration in the Neoclassical Bank of England in Threadneedle Street, London, and the Baroque master Bernini's colonnade at St. Peter's Piazza in Rome. Inside, McKim modeled the vast waiting room on the Roman Baths of Caracalla. When the station opened in 1910, 100,000 people turned out to watch the first trains there.

Burnham's firm designed Union Station in Washington: Beaux-Arts at perhaps its finest and grandest. Built to serve all seven railroad lines entering the capital, the new station went up on filled land along the edge of a tenement district known as Swampoodle. White and massive it loomed, the barrel-vaulted Main Hall— a waiting room with mahogany benches and ticketing facilities—rising nine stories high. The Main Hall opened onto the noble train concourse, 760 feet long, 130 feet wide, with an arched and vaulted roof. Decorative iron gateways led to thirty train platforms.

The early years of the last century saw, too, the last of the great train sheds, marvels of Victorian engineering. The single-span arched shed at Burnham's Union (later Pennsylvania) Station in Pittsburgh, completed in 1901, extended 247 feet in width. The station itself rose twelve stories high. Out front, a curved carriage concourse led to an outdoor rotunda with ornate French-inspired decoration prosaically known as the "cabstand." The Pittsburgh train shed came down in 1947. By then, the simpler, less expensive Bush shed and its successor, the still more economical butterfly shelters, had supplanted the great glass-and-iron sheds of the

nineteenth century. At Boston's South Station (1898), a triple-arched shed originally extended from the Classical Revival head house. By 1930 butterfly sheds provided partial cover for the twenty-eight stub-end tracks that terminated at South Station.

These colossal new buildings were deeply considered projects. "Architects and corporations were perfectly aware that they were subordinating economy and convenience to other values; but they held these other values to be of more lasting significance," wrote Meeks. "The designers accepted as valid the classic conception that public buildings should be supremely impressive. They adopted the classic means: fine materials, uniform color, colossal scale, and a comparatively narrow range of form. They gave long and careful thought to the refinement and perfection of the design and eschewed self-expression." With the advantage of hindsight, there is something almost touching about the misplaced optimism of the railroad magnates who commissioned the Beaux-Arts station-monuments. Even as new stations were opening to great fanfare in Worcester, Massachusetts (1911), Kansas City (1914), Jacksonville, Florida (1921), and elsewhere, early signs of the long decline of the railroad lines were manifest. The architects and engineers designed the Kansas City terminal,

Below: *Converted to reuse as a conference center, the classical lines of this Ottawa terminal are strongly contrasted against the modern office building in the background.*

for example, to handle 350 trains per day. At the peak of traffic in 1917, 218 trains per day stopped here. Before too long, the great gleaming metropolitan stations would be practical and psychological liabilities for their owners.

While Beaux-Arts dominated, there were, of course, picturesque survivals into the twentieth century. The president of the New York, New Haven & Hartford, so the story goes, had been so impressed by a recent tour of Italy that he ordered up a campanile for the line's new station in Waterbury, Connecticut. The firm of McKim, Mead and White dutifully, but belatedly, added a 245-foot-high bell tower to the two-story Renaissance Revival design. Not everyone approved of the afterthought: "The tower is so awkwardly superimposed that one wonders if the architects intended to demonstrate the folly of amateur interference," Meeks remarked on a wry note.

Spanish Colonial Revival designs persisted here and there, especially in the South and West, although one appeared, rather surprisingly, in Westerly, Rhode Island, where in 1912 a brick-and-stucco Spanish-style building replaced the original wooden depot of 1837. A large octagonal dome surmounted the beige-brick Spanish Revival Union Depot in Mobile, Alabama, opened in 1907. Architect M.A. Griffith's design for the Atlantic Coast Line station in Orlando,

Florida, showed the influence of the early Spanish architecture of Florida and the Southwest. Completed in 1927, the station featured a trackside colonnade, with twin bell towers flanking a wide arched entryway.

The Pennsylvania Railroad commissioned the last of the great Neoclassical monuments, 30th Street Station in Philadelphia, which opened in 1930. The façade, facing the Schuylkill River and clad in Alabama limestone, featured 71-foot-high Corinthian columns. The interior housed the PRR's regional offices and contained two levels for trains, a set of upper platforms for commuter services and underground ones for long-distance lines. Gilded marble columns, a marble floor and a 98-foot-high coffered ceiling in red, cream and gold added luxury to the interior.

The railroad historian John F. Stover identified the year 1916 as "marking the end of the golden age of railroading." The U.S. railroad network reached its all-time high that year, with 254,000 miles of track in service. At the same time, the first substantial eliminations of passenger service were occurring as competing forms of transportation began to emerge. Congress passed the Federal Road Aid Act in 1916, a measure that provided highway construction grants to the states. Henry Ford's Model T had appeared in 1908, and by 1916 private automobile registrations reached 3.3 million. By the end of the 1920s, 25 million private cars would be cruising America's expanding highway system.

By then, too, a fledgling airline network had developed. The U.S. Post Office introduced airmail service between New York and Washington in 1918 and established a transcontinental airmail route in the mid-1920s. By 1930 the airlines were carrying a growing number of passengers, too. Motor buses captured 18 percent of intercity passenger traffic in 1930. Trucks hauled an increasing share of the nation's agricultural produce. Pipelines cut into the railroads' business in liquid freight. "The convenience of the truck, the speed of the airline, the economy of the bus and the cheap reliability of the pipeline contrived to reduce the railroad's share of the nation's transportation pie," wrote Stover.

Below: *Multiple tracks led into the train shed of the Pennsylvania Railroad's Broad Street Station, Philadelphia. The station, which once served 160 trains a day, fell to the wrecker's ball in 1952.*

Still, for some years the declines were more real than apparent. Some railroads invested heavily in improved services. The Baltimore & Ohio introduced air-conditioned passenger cars in 1931. In 1934 the first diesel/electric locomotives, more cost-efficient and reliable than steamers, entered into railroad service. Diesel power and streamlining made for faster, more reliable and more comfortable trains. The Burlington's torpedo-like "Zephyr," for example, averaged 77.6mph on a nonstop run from Chicago to Denver in May 1934. Even during the Great Depression of the 1930s, as the railroads discontinued passenger services and put out the lights in hundreds of smaller depots, the great railroad companies continued to build.

The architect Louis Sullivan had been uneasily associated with Daniel Burnham on the World's Columbian Exposition; he accused Burnham and his followers of adopting a "bogus antique" style for the White City that delayed the development of modernist functionalism in America. Sullivan, the first Modern American architect, died in relative obscurity in 1924. Within a few years of his passing, the functionalists' day had come, not least in design of the last generation of railroad stations built in the United States and Canada.

The new style reduced, or even eliminated, ornamentation. Early functional designs were sternly geometric, though as time passed domes and other curved forms reappeared and ornamentation grew more elaborate. Along with the severe designs that marked the era of railroad economizing after Stover's benchmark year of 1916 came other functional if impersonal efficiencies: automatically opening doors, escalators, lunch counters or cafeterias rather than full-service restaurants, public address systems instead of trainboards.

Philadelphia architect Paul Philippe Cret made curves the leading feature of the new Union Terminal in Cincinnati, begun in 1929. The station, which replaced several depots scattered about the city when it opened in 1933, had an arched façade that contemporaries compared to a radio cabinet of the Art Deco era. It rose

on a marshland site a mile from the central city, with vast parking lots all around—"the railway station as airport," according to Richards and MacKenzie. In the rotunda and concourse beyond the 200-foot-wide arched entrance, elaborate mosaics depicted local and national historical themes.

The long-delayed Central Terminal in Buffalo, New York, the midpoint on the New York Central's New York-Chicago main line, opened on the city's outskirts in 1930. An office tower rose 271 feet high next to the barrel-vaulted terminal, which also suggested the curved top of a contemporary radio cabinet. The grand concourse, more than 400 feet long, featured Art Deco-style ornamentation. Cleveland's Union Terminal, with its fifty-two-story office skyscraper, then the tallest building west of New York City, opened in 1930. The Fred Harvey Company managed the terminal's complex of shops and restaurants. In Fort Worth, Texas, the Texas & Pacific put up a thirteen-story passenger station and office building (1931) in granite, limestone and brick, with Art Deco detailing. The geometrical Union Station in Omaha also opened in 1931. In spite of its Art Deco exterior, some observers suggested, unkindly, that it most resembled a mausoleum.

Above: *Sailors head for their trains in this World War II scene at 30th Street Station in Philadelphia. The Pennsylvania Railroad opened the station, a grand Neoclassical pile overlooking the Schuylkill River, in 1933.*

Railroads continued to build into the 1940s and '50s. The modernist station at Burlington, Iowa, which opened in 1944, featured a lounge that townsfolk regarded as the most comfortable public room in the community. With its "closed boxes" design, Meeks rated Burlington as "one of the best recent American stations." New depots opened in Toledo, Ohio, in 1950 and in New Orleans in 1954.

Still, these were isolated additions to a steadily contracting landscape of railroad buildings. Highway and air traffic continued to grow. In 1940 airlines carried 3 percent of intercity passenger traffic. Between 1951 and 1956, American railroads eliminated nearly 1,300 trains. In 1957, for the first time, more passengers traveled by air than by rail. In Indianapolis, thirty-two trains a day called at Union Station in 1959, down from 184 trains a day a half-century earlier. In the early 1960s, Maine became the first of the continental United States to be totally deprived of railroad passenger service.

The essayist E.B. White, perhaps Maine's best-known part-time resident during the middle decades of the twentieth century, blamed the railroads themselves for much of their plight. He saw their conservatism as the problem, a hidebound and customer-repellent approach reflected even in the unfriendly design of the Maine passenger stations he stubbornly continued to frequent.

"Some of the station houses were so solidly built they still stand, monuments to darkness and decay," White wrote in "The Railroad," an essay of 1960. "The depot at Bangor, built in 1907, is a notable example of a railroad's addiction to the glorious past. Give it bars at the windows and it could as well be a federal penitentiary. Give it a moat with a drawbridge and it could be the castle where the baron lives."

Progressive thinking and fast expresses like the Burlington's "Zephyr" were equally rare during the twilight years of the railroads. White, who grew up in the New York City suburb of Mount Vernon, made his first rail journey to Maine in 1905. His family, a large one, traveled by Pullman overnight sleeper at a stately average pace of 30–35mph, with plenty of halts to

discharge and take on passengers, express packages and mail along the way. A half-century later, during the last days of railroad passenger service between New York City and Bangor, the average speed remained about the same, while automobiles raced down America's new four-lane superhighways at rates of 70mph and more and jet aircraft thundered across the sky at a near-supersonic 500mph.

"A train on its leisurely course often reminds me of a boy who has been sent on an errand," White mused; "the train gets there eventually, and so does the boy, but after what adventures, what amusing distractions and excursions, what fruitful dawdling! A railroad has a thousand and one things on its mind, all of them worthy, many of them enchanting, but none of them conducive to swift passage for a seated customer."

If the railroads were complicit in their own demise, public policymakers accelerated the process of decay. Indirect subsidies massive enough to make the Central Pacific's Big Four blush supported the automotive and airline industries. State and federal governments built highways while taxing railroads at high rates. In 1956 city-owned Midway Airport in Chicago

Above: *The Santa Fe passenger depot at Riverside, California, opened in 1927 with an updated and streamlined Pueblo look. Passenger service ended in 1971 and the station became part of a redevelopment project.*

Opposite, above: *The 1909 Santa Fe depot at Weatherford, Texas, west of Fort Worth, survived the decline of the railroads to become a Chamber of Commerce office.*

Opposite, below: *A long parklike avenue approached the main entrance of the concrete-and-steel dome of Cincinnati's curvaceous Union Terminal (1933).*

PENNSYLVANIA R.R. UNION STATION BURLINGTON ROUTE | THE ALTON ROAD | MILWAUKEE R.R.

...on Station   CHICAGO, ILL.
                                                         C-5

Above: *Chicago's Union Station (1913–25) featured a Neoclassical head house of Indiana limestone that resembled Pennsylvania Station in New York City. Though wreckers knocked down the fine concourse in 1969, Union Station still serves long-distance and commuter passengers.*

paid nothing in property taxes; the bill for Union Station (opened in 1925) totaled $900,000. In the same year, the federal Interstate Highway Act launched construction of a national system of four-lane limited access highways, including I-95 from Maine to Florida, the throughway that helped drive White's beloved Maine Central and Bangor & Aroostook out of business.

The wholesale destruction of railroad stations accompanied the decline of railroad passenger service. In an act of high vandalism, the Pennsylvania Railroad sold the "air rights" to Pennsylvania Station in New York City and in 1963 began demolition of the Beaux-Arts masterpiece. The Madison Square Garden sports arena rose upon the site, driving the new station, as functional as ever a 1930s Modern architect could wish, entirely underground.

Hundreds, even thousands, of depots were demolished. In 1916 there were 85,000 passenger and combination passenger-freight stations in the United States. In the last decade of the century, by historian Janet Greenstein Potter's estimate, fewer than 12,000 survived. Municipalities sacrificed decrepit trackside structures in firefighting exercises. Charming gingerbread-style stations at Ardmore, Bryn Mawr and Paoli were knocked down successively along Philadelphia's main line in the 1950s, replaced by nondescript buildings in dull brick. Grand Central Station in Chicago, built in 1890 with a 247-foot-high brick clock tower, came down in 1970. The Italianate red-brick Queen City

Railroad Station and Hotel in Cumberland, Maryland, built for the venerable B&O in 1872, fell in 1972. A prefabricated depot replaced the Cumberland monument, which would join Pennsylvania Station as a poster building for wanton destruction. The wrecker's ball claimed San Francisco's Mission-style Southern Pacific Station at Third and Townsend, completed in 1915, in 1975–77.

Union Station in Portland, Maine, opened in 1888 with a 138-foot-tall Chateauesque clock tower, a none-too-subtle prod to punctuality for passengers of the Boston & Maine, the Maine Central, the Portland and Ogdensburg and the Portland & Rochester Railroads. Wreckers dismantled the station in August 1961, and a shopping center fills the site today. In May of the following year, E.B. White added a mournful postscript to "The Railroad."

"Death came quickly to the railroads of Maine," he wrote. "The passenger trains not only disappeared 'in my lifetime,' they disappeared in what seemed like a trice. The trains are gone, the station houses are gone. I was watching television one day and saw the tower of Portland's Union Station fall over, struck down by a large steel ball swinging from the boom of a crane. I could feel the blow in the pit of my stomach."

It seemed so final. But something of a resurrection of railroad passenger service lay in the not-so-distant future. Congress knocked together the National Railroad Passenger Corporation—Amtrak—in 1971 out of the ruins of the great railroad lines. Amtrak has been up and down, but at least the shadow of a national passenger network survives. There is every prospect, too, that the cars will return even to Maine, at least as far as Portland, early in the new century. And though much of America's railroad heritage has been heedlessly destroyed, much of value remains. The destruction of Pennsylvania Station mobilized the preservationists. Congress passed the National Historic Preservation Act in 1966, and subsequent legislation offered incentives for saving and restoring old depots and adapting them for new uses. Though these measures failed to save dozens of smaller stations that disappeared in the 1970s, there were at the same time a number of quite spectacular successes.

Preservationists won a close-run battle to save Henry Hobson Richardson's Union Station in New London, Connecticut, in the 1970s. Developers converted Daniel H. Burnham's Pennsylvania Station in Pittsburgh into apartments. St. Louis's magnificent Romanesque Union Station houses a hotel, restaurants and shops as well as its railroad services. The Richardsonian Romanesque depot in Battle Creek, Michigan, became a restaurant.

The city of Danbury, Connecticut, converted the 1903 Union Station there into a railroad museum in the 1990s. South Station in Boston, which saw the first trains arrive and depart on New Year's Day 1899, served Amtrak long-distance and MBTA commuter trains in 1999 and remained one of America's busiest terminals. Washington's monumental Union Station, beautifully restored and rededicated in 1988, offers a range of restaurants, shops and extensive facilities for special events as well as Amtrak and commuter rail services.

In Durham, New Hampshire, students of the University of New Hampshire operate a dairy bar and grill in the old Boston & Maine station, built in 1896 in East Lynn, Massachusetts, and moved to Durham in 1910. The 1856 depot at Dover, Delaware, became a courthouse in the 1970s. Newark's Art Deco Pennsylvania Station of 1935, restored in the mid-1980s as part of the Northeast Corridor Improvement Project, still serves Amtrak and New Jersey commuters.

Preservationists restored New York's Grand Central to its original glory during the 1990s. Indianapolis rededicated its Romanesque Union Station as a retail center and hotel in 1986, ninety-eight years after it opened. Kansas City's Beaux-Arts Union Station of 1914 houses a science museum today. The elegant Spanish Colonial Revival-style depot in Claremont, California, built for the Atchison, Topeka & Santa Fe Railway in 1927 and restored in 1992, is a stop on the Los Angeles region's Metrolink commuter rail line.

The successes, though, are bittersweet. For most travelers, other than commuters into metropolitan centers, the rails exist as a lesser transportation alternative, a third or fourth option. Surviving stations are monuments to a vanished age, separate, chilly, sometimes seeming as remote from everyday life as an equestrian statue in a park. Even the preservationists recognize that something vital is missing:

"And yet—and yet—for all this earnest and worthy work of conservation, the life has gone irrevocably out of these stations," Richards and MacKenzie acknowledged. "Without the ebb and flow of passengers, the arrival and departure of trains, they have in a very real sense ceased to be. For steam was the breath which animated them, and that breath has been stilled."

Below: *Passengers collect in Grand Central Terminal's magnificent main concourse. Architectural historian Carroll Meeks called Grand Central "one of the outstandingly successful stations of history."*

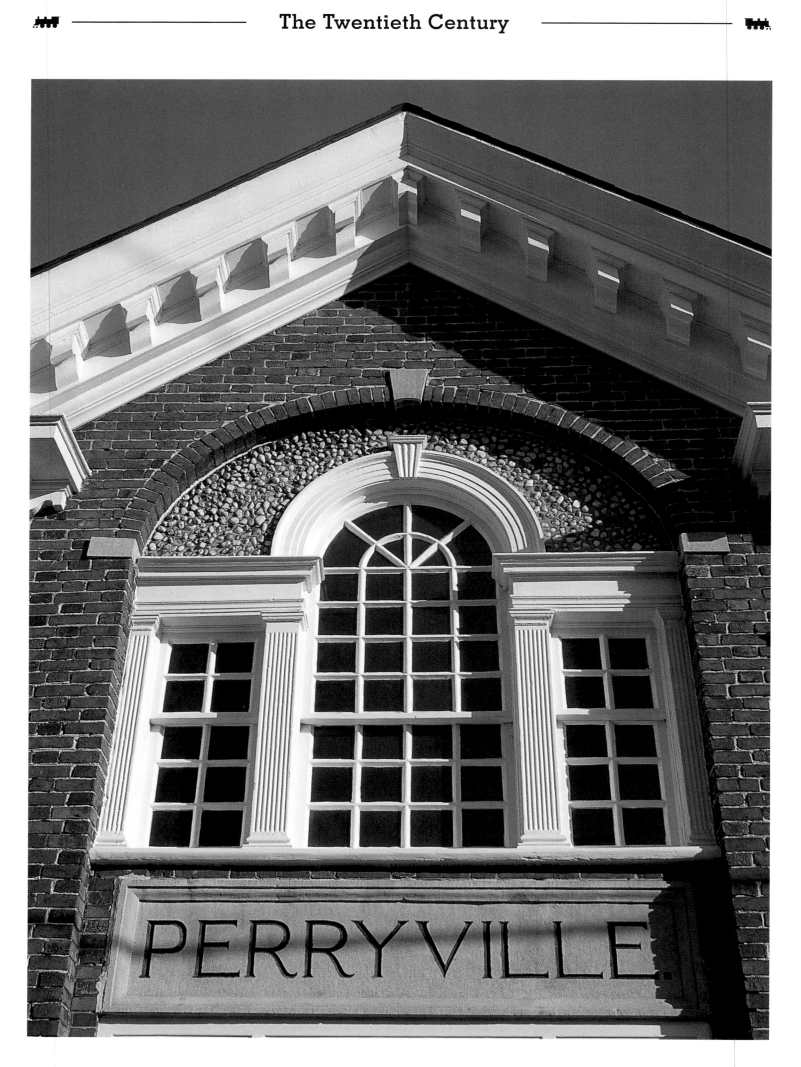

Colonial Revival at Perryville, Maryland

Previous pages

The Philadelphia, Baltimore & Washington Railroad opened the Colonial Revival station at Perryville, Maryland, in 1905. A long canopy divided the second-story fanlights from the three-section windows on the ground floor. Cornice, Palladian windows and the Maryland station's name etched in stone form a graceful group.

An indestructible-looking bridge carried Philadelphia, Washington & Baltimore passenger trains over the Susquehanna River at Perryville.

Baltimore's Railroad Heritage *Opposite and below*

Locomotives built up steam at Baltimore's Neoclassical Union Station in 1914 (below). Restored in the 1980s, the 1911 building is now known as Pennsylvania Station.

Baltimore's Romanesque Mount Royal Station (1896) is shown on the opposite page in the mid-1950s, near the end of its career as a Baltimore & Ohio passenger terminal. The Maryland Art Institute converted the building into an art school annex in the 1960s.

Art Deco in Los Angeles

Details from the Union Passenger Terminal in Los Angeles (1939) illustrate its harmonious blend of traditional Spanish and Modernist Art Deco forms. A clocktower (right) rises alongside the mosaic-tiled arched entrance to the station, which was constructed of steel clad in concrete. Several architects collaborated on the building; Mary Colter designed the restaurant and other interior spaces. The station continues in use and retains many of its original interior features.

Spanish Influences in California *Right and below*
The Southern Pacific Railroad opened its Mission-style
station (below) in San Francisco in 1915, replacing an
earthquake-shattered depot on the same site at Third and
Townsend streets. The building was demolished in 1975. At
right, dude ranchers wait on the platform in this winter scene
at the passenger station serving the desert resort of Palm
Springs, California.

Union Station, Denver

Right

A neon addition to the Beaux-Arts façade of Denver's Union Station (1881; façade 1915) exhorts Coloradans to travel by rail. Note the tiny Amtrak logo at the bottom center of the photo.

A Lost Jewel

The distinguished architect Charles McKim modeled the vast waiting room (opposite) of Pennsylvania Station in New York City (1910) on the Roman Baths of Caracalla. The colonnaded pink-toned granite building was among the Big Apple's best-loved twentieth-century landmarks until its highly controversial demolition in 1963. At right, the station's Savarin Restaurant is shown ready for a crush of diners in this photograph from April 1930. Below, an arched steel-framed entryway led to the general waiting room at Pennsylvania Station.

Philadelphia's 30th Street Station *Above*
A bronze and glass lantern and the Pennsylvania Railroad's
keystone logo are among the painstakingly restored
ornamental details of 30th Street Station (originally named
Pennsylvania Station) in Philadelphia (1933). This heavily
trafficked hub in the hometown of the Pennsy was overhauled
in the late 1980s by Amtrak.

Manhattan's *Grande Dame* *Right*
Restored during the 1990s, the Main Concourse at venerable
Grand Central Terminal (1903–13) glows with renewed
vitality and purpose in its role as a noble gateway to the city.
Sweeping marble staircases at either end of the concourse and
an elaborate zodiac on the high curved ceiling distinguish this
magnificent interior.

Empire Rooflines *Opposite*

The Union Pacific's French Renaissance Revival station in Salt Lake City (opposite, above) dates from 1909. The building is more ornate than most UP depots: the lower story is clad in sandstone and the upper, in brick, while ornamental details include decorative metalwork and circular-shaped dormers set into the Mansard roof. The state of Utah took possession of the depot in the late 1980s. Opposite, below, the Union Pacific transfer depot at Council Bluffs, Iowa, the staging place for transcontinental railroad journeys since the advent of cross-country service in 1869.

The Railway Writ Large *Above*

Toronto's monumental Union Station, designed on formal Classical lines, opened in 1927. As the automobiles lined up in front suggest, railroads in Canada and the United States were already facing competition that would drive them into a long, steady and permanent decline, though many of the continent's largest cities have maintained efficient rail services for commuters to combat inner-city traffic congestion.

Texas Contrasts *Above and opposite, above*
The Beaux-Arts Union Station in Dallas (above) opened in 1916 on a site overlooking Ferris Plaza. Reunion Tower rises to dramatic effect behind the station. Amtrak still uses the original Union Station waiting room. Opposite, above, Houston's functional Union Station, part depot, part office block, dates from 1911–12. As many as 10,000 Houstonians turned out for the dedication gala in 1911.

Georgian Revival *Opposite, below*
The Georgian Revival station in Vicksburg, Mississippi, opened in 1907, saw the last passenger train pull away from the platform in 1950. The building subsequently housed a restaurant and shops.

Scenes from the Interior *Overleaf*
Travelers queue up to complete "through" train arrangements in this scene from the 1930s (page 138, top), repeated in station waiting rooms across the United States and Canada. Below, baggage handlers sort through steamer trunks, valises and packages below decks of the Union Passenger Terminal in Los Angeles (see pages 126-127).

On page 139, a well-dressed family collects baggage checks from a Southern Pacific porter in San Francisco in this 1938 promotional photo.

Italian Renaissance, Utah Style *Left*

A traveler passing through Ogden, Utah, could well be impressed by its 1924 Union Depot, designed by a Los Angeles firm in the Italian Renaissance Revival style. The depot combined pink and buff-colored brick to resemble Cordova tile. Wrought-iron chandeliers and blue mosaic tile ornament the entrance porches to what is now a mixed-use civic center.

Chateau Style, Newfoundland *Above*

The dressed-stone station at St. John's, Newfoundland, had a steeply pitched metal roof designed on Chateauesque lines, the better for shedding northern snows.

Wisconsin Commuting *Left*

The Chicago & Northwestern Railroad's passenger depot in Green Bay, Wisconsin (1899), boasted a towering campanile with four clock faces. The long platform canopy shelters passengers from the sleets and snows of Green Bay.

BIBLIOGRAPHY

Alexander, Edwin P. *Down at the Depot*. New York: Clarkson N. Potter Inc., 1970.

Berg, Walter G. *Buildings and Structures of American Railroads*. New York: John Wiley & Sons, 1892.

Dickens, Charles. *American Notes*. Boston: Estes and Lauriat, 1890 ed.

Dodge, Grenville. *How We Built the Union Pacific Railway*. Ann Arbor, Mich.: University Microfilms, 1966 reprint of 1910 edition.

Douglas, George H. *All Aboard: The Railroad in American Life*. New York: Paragon House, 1992.

Emerson, Ralph Waldo. *Essays and Lectures*. New York: Library of America, 1983.

Gordon, Sarah. *Passage to Union: How the Railroads Transformed American Life*. Chicago: Ivan R. Dee, 1996.

Grow, Lawrence, ed. *Waiting for the 5:05: Terminal, Station and Depot in America*. New York: Main Street/Universe Books, 1977.

Holbrook, Stewart H. *The Story of American Railroads*. New York: Crown, 1947.

Hubbard, Freeman. *Encyclopedia of North American Railroading*. New York: McGraw Hill, 1981.

Marshall, James. *Santa Fe: The Railroad that Built an Empire*. New York: Random House, 1945.

Meeks, Carroll. *The Railroad Station: An Architectural History*. New Haven: Yale University Press, 1956.

Potter, Janet Greenstein. *Great American Railroad Stations*. New York: John Wiley & Sons, 1996.

Richards, Jeffrey and John M. MacKenzie. *The Railway Station: A Social History*. New York: Oxford University Press, 1986.

Solomon, Brian. *Railroad Stations*. New York: Friedman/Fairfax Publishers, 1998.

Stover, John F. *American Railroads*. Chicago: University of Chicago Press, 1961.

Ward, James A. *Railroads and the Character of America, 1820–1887*. Knoxville: University of Tennessee Press, 1986.

White, E.B. "The Railroad," in *The Essays of E.B. White*. New York: HarperPerennial, 1992.

ACKNOWLEDGMENTS

The publisher would like to thank the following individuals for their assistance in the preparation of this book: Robin Langley Sommer and Sara Hunt, editors; Nicola J. Gillies, picture researcher; Charles J. Ziga, art director; Nikki L. Fesak, graphic designer; Lisa Langone Desautels, indexer; and the following people for their research, advice and general assistance: Marty Azola, Bill Botorff, Anne Calhoun, Nancy Finlay, Jerry Jordak, Don D. Snoddy, Bill Whitaker.